T0307979

Geographies of Digital Exclusion

'Conceptually rich and well-illustrated, this is a valuable analysis of data power at the global scale.'
—Professor Rob Kitchin, Maynooth University

'An enlightening and accessible introduction to digital geographies and why they are important to our understanding of digital exclusion.'
—Alex Singleton, Professor of Geographic Information Science, University of Liverpool

'Demonstrates how so much digital data is sourced from a very limited range of geographical locations and laboured over in various ways, and what difference this makes to the information about places on platforms like OpenStreetMap, Google Maps and Wikipedia.'
—Gillian Rose, Professor of Human Geography, School of Geography and the Environment, University of Oxford

'Systematic, sobering, yet uplifting, this volume makes the convincing case that digital transformation is not the end of geography, nor is it an equaliser for the diverse cultures and peoples across the globe.'
—Jack Linchuan Qiu, Professor at the Department of Communications and New Media, National University of Singapore

'An important and insightful book. Graham and Dittus eloquently map, measure and critically interrogate digital geographies in a way that forces us to reckon with their power and politics, the injustices they incur, and how we might imagine alternatives.'
—Professor Lina Dencik, Co-Director of the Data Justice Lab, Cardiff University

'A must read for those deeply concerned about long hidden people and places who have been marginalised in the politics of place-making, including within digital worlds like Wikipedia and Google.'
—Payal Arora, author of *The Next Billion Users* and Co-Founder of FemLab.Co

Radical Geography

Series Editors:
Danny Dorling, Matthew T. Huber and Jenny Pickerill
Former editor: Kate Derickson

Also available:

Disarming Doomsday:
The Human Impact of Nuclear Weapons since Hiroshima
Becky Alexis-Martin

Unlocking Sustainable Cities:
A Manifesto for Real Change
Paul Chatterton

In Their Place:
The Imagined Geographies of Poverty
Stephen Crossley

Making Workers:
Radical Geographies of Education
Katharyne Mitchell

Space Invaders:
Radical Geographies of Protest
Paul Routledge

Data Power:
Radical Geographies of Control and Resistance
Jim E. Thatcher and Craig M. Dalton

New Borders:
Migration, Hotspots and the European Superstate
Antonis Vradis, Evie Papada, Joe Painter and Anna Papoutsi

Geographies of Digital Exclusion

Data and Inequality

Mark Graham and Martin Dittus

First published 2022 by Pluto Press
New Wing, Somerset House, Strand, London WC2R 1LA

www.plutobooks.com

Copyright © Mark Graham and Martin Dittus 2022

The right of Mark Graham and Martin Dittus to be identified as the authors
of this work has been asserted in accordance with the Copyright, Designs and
Patents Act 1988.

British Library Cataloguing in Publication Data
A catalogue record for this book is available from the British Library

ISBN   978 0 7453 4019 7   Hardback
ISBN   978 0 7453 4018 0   Paperback
ISBN   978 1 786807 41 0   PDF
ISBN   978 1 786807 42 7   EPUB

Typeset by Stanford DTP Services, Northampton, England

Simultaneously printed in the United Kingdom and United States of America

Contents

Figures

Series Preface

The Radical Geography series consists of accessible books which use geographical perspectives to understand issues of social and political concern. These short books include critiques of existing government policies and alternatives to staid ways of thinking about our societies. They feature stories of radical social and political activism, guides to achieving change, and arguments about why we need to think differently on many contemporary issues if we are to live better together on this planet.

A geographical perspective involves seeing the connections within and between places, as well as considering the role of space and scale to develop a new and better understanding of current problems. Written largely by academic geographers, books in the series deliberately target issues of political, environmental and social concern. The series showcases clear explications of geographical approaches to social problems, and it has a particular interest in action currently being undertaken to achieve positive change that is radical, achievable, real and relevant.

The target audience ranges from undergraduates to experienced scholars, as well as from activists to conventional policy-makers, but these books are also for people interested in the world who do not already have a radical outlook and who want to be engaged and informed by a short, well written and thought-provoking book.

Danny Dorling, Matthew T. Huber and Jenny Pickerill
Series Editors

Acknowledgements

This work in this book is inspired, encouraged and motivated by a few key people and projects. We would like to acknowledge: Matt Zook for his pioneering work in the field of digital geography that provided a foundation for us to pursue our own work in this area; the rest of the Floating Sheep Collective (Taylor Shelton, Monica Stephens, Ate Poorthuis) for making internet geography both critical and fun; Bernie Hogan, Ilhem Allagui, Ralph Straumann, Ahmed Medhat, Sanna Ojanperä, Ali Frihida, Claudio Calvino, Stefano De Sabbata, Richard Farmbrough, Heather Ford, Frederike Kaltheuner, David Palfrey, Gavin Bailey, Kalina Bontcheva, Taha Yasseri and Clarence Singleton for being star collaborators on our earlier 'Uneven Openness' project: Whose Knowledge – in particular, Adele Vrana, Anasuya Sengupta, Claudia Pozo and Siko Bouterse – whose efforts to centre the knowledge of marginalised communities (the majority of the world) on the internet are already world-changing and world-improving, sometimes quietly and sometimes not so quietly; Sneha Puthiya Purayil and Sumandro Chattapadhyay at the Centre for Internet & Society; Bill Dutton, Vicki Nash, Viktor Mayer-Schönberger and Helen Margetts for encouraging and supporting our work at the OII for over a decade; Cailean Osborne, at the Centre for Data Ethics & Innovation; Licia Capra, Pete Masters, Andrew Braye, Melanie Eckle and countless others who have helped shape Martin's previous research on the Humanitarian OpenStreetMap Team; Rob Kitchin, Agnieszka Leszczynski and Matt Wilson for their always inspiring contributions at AAG meetings; and, last but not least, the wonderful DPhil students that we've had the privilege of working with at the OII: Heather Ford for her pathbreaking work on representation in Wikipedia; Joe Shaw for driving forwards our thinking into digital rights to the city; Sanna Ojanperä and Khairunnisa Haji Ibrahim for their careful and committed work into digital inequalities; and Margie Cheesman, Fabian Ferrari and Marie-Therese Png for critically thinking through the political economy of digital infrastructures. We've learnt a lot from each of you, and thanks for keeping our compass pointed in the right direction.

We have deeply benefited from the conversations, debates and political engagements that the authors have engaged in as part of the Fairwork and Geonet projects based at the Oxford Internet Institute, University of Oxford. Thank you very much to Amir Anwar, Fabian Braeseman, Stefano De Sabbata, Chris Foster, Sanna Ojanperä, Fabian Stephany, Ralph Straumann, Michel Wahome, Daniel Abs, Iftikhar Ahmad, María Belén Albornoz, Moritz Altenried, Paula Alves, Oğuz Alyanak, Branka Andjelkovic, Thomas Anning-Dorson, Arturo Arriagada, Daniel Arubayi, Tat Chor Au-Yeung, Alessio Bertolini, Louise Bezuidenhout, Gautam Bhatia, Richard Boateng, Manuela Bojadzijev, Macarena Bonhomme, Maren Borkert, Joseph Budu, Rodrigo Carelli, Henry Chavez, Sonata Cepik, Aradhana Cherupara Vadekkethil, Chris King Chi Chan, Matthew Cole, Paska Darmawan, Markieta Domecka, Darcy du Toit, Veena Dubal, Trevilliana Eka Putri, Fabian Ferrari, Patrick Feuerstein, Roseli Figaro, Milena Franke, Sandra Fredman, Pia Garavaglia, Farah Ghazal, Anita Ghazi Rahman, Shikoh Gitau, Slobodan Golusin, Markus Griesser, Rafael Grohman, Martin Gruber-Risak, Sayema Haque Bidisha, Khadiga Hassan, Richard Heeks, Mabel Rocío Hernández Díaz, Luis Jorge Hernández Flores, Benjamin Herr, Salma Hindy, Kelle Howson, Francisco Ibáñez, Sehrish Irfan, Tanja Jakobi, Athar Jameel, Hannah Johnston, Srujana Katta, Maja Kovac, Martin Krzywdzinski, Larry Kwan, Sebastian Lew, Jorge Leyton, Melissa Malala, Oscar Javier Maldonado, Shabana Malik, Laura Clemencia Mantilla León, Claudia Marà, Évilin Matos, Sabrina Mustabin Jaigirdar, Tasnim Mustaque, Baraka Mwaura, Mounika Neerukonda, Sidra Nizamuddin, Thando Nkohla-Ramunenyiwa, Sanna Ojanperä, Caroline Omware, Adel Osama, Balaji Parthasarathy, Leonhard Plank, Valeria Pulignano, Jack Qui, Ananya Raihan, Pablo Aguera Reneses, Nabiyla Risfa Izzati, Nagla Rizk, Cheryll Ruth Soriano, Nancy Salem, Julice Salvagni, Derly Yohanna Sánchez Vargas, Kanikka Sersia, Murali Shanmugavelan, Shanza Sohail, Janaki Srinivasan, Shelly Steward, Zuly Bibiana Suárez Morales, Sophie Sun, David Sutcliffe, Pradyumna Taduri, Kristin Thompson, Pitso Tsibolane, Anna Tsui, Funda Ustek-Spilda, Jean-Paul Van Belle, Laura Vogel, Zoya Waheed, Jing Wang, Robbie Warin, Nadine Weheba and Yihan Zhu.

A big thanks to the organisers and attendees at events and workshops whose engagement with our early material helped us develop it further: The Geonet Digital | Economy | Africa Conference 2018 in Johannesburg; Data Justice 2018 in Cardiff; Decolonising the Internet 2018 in Cape Town, in particular Kelly Foster and Christel Steigenberger;

Wikimania 2018 in Cape Town, in particular Bobby Shabangu, Josh Lim, Frikan Erwee, Douglas Scott, Jens Ohlig, Lea Voget, and Lydia Pintscher; Worlds of Wikimedia 2019 in Sydney, in particular Bunty Avieson and team; State of the Map 2019 in Heidelberg; HOT Summit 2019 in Heidelberg; WikiArabia 2019 in Marrakech, in particular Ezarraf Noureddine, Vasanthi Hargyono, Asaf Bartov, Marc Miquel-Ribé, Farah Mustaklem; Decolonizing The Internet's Languages at MozFest 2019 in London; all of the participants in our Wikipedia in the Middle East workshops in Cairo and Amman; and, finally, the participants at our RGS-IBG 2018 workshop in Cardiff, titled 'Digital Representations of Place: Urban Overlays and Digital Justice', including speakers Gillian Rose, Muki Haklay, Rob Kitchin and Yu-Shan Tseng, as well as countless others who provided thoughtful reflections on the inequities inherent in digital representation.

A huge thank you to everyone who offered perspectives, critique and advice regarding work contained in earlier drafts of this book, including: Danny Dorling, Mandana Seyfeddinipur, Ben Drury, David 'Mapmaker' Garcia, Matt Wilson, Ralph Straumann, Taha Yasseri and Nancy Salem. Special thanks also to Nancy Salem and David Sutcliffe for their invaluable edits and comments at the final stage of the book.

We are grateful to the volunteer translators for our research of Google Maps in Chapter 5, including: Anasuya Sengupta, ashashyou, Babalwa Tembeni, Bonface Witaba, Bruno Lincoln, Buntubonke Mzondo, Busisiwe Moloi, Can Liu, Champ Wu, Dror Kamir, Elisa Pannini, Emaliana Kasmuri, Emerson Leandro Monteiro, Farah Mustaklem, Frikan Erwee, Gabriel Eugênio Aquino Diedrich, Irene Poetranto, Laure Joanny, Nduta Mugo, R. Fanelwa Ajayi, Ruben De Smet, Sephora Mianda, Xavier Romero-Vidal and everyone who helped promote our call for translators.

Thank you to The Alan Turing Institute for providing us with hotdesks and WiFi in central London, and to David Castle and Pluto for their trust and patience as we prepared our manuscript.

Parts of the book are reproductions and reworkings of earlier publications in the *Annals of the Association of American Geographers*, *Geo* and *Wired*.

Finally, thank you to Adel El Zaim, Matthew Smith, Laurent Elder, Gehane Said and Nola Haddadian of the IDRC for supporting our earlier research on the geographies of Wikipedia. Our research in this book was primarily funded by the Leverhulme Prize (PLP-2016-155) and

Whose Knowledge. Mark Graham is partially funded as a Turing Fellow under Turing Award Number TU/B/000042. This work was also made possible through funding from the European Research Council under the European Union's Seventh Framework Programme for Research and Technological Development (FP/2007–2013)/ERC Grant Agreement No. 335716.

1

We All Are Digital Geographers

Governments of the Industrial World, you weary giants of flesh and steel, I come from Cyberspace, the new home of Mind. On behalf of the future, I ask you of the past to leave us alone. You are not welcome among us. You have no sovereignty where we gather.

We have no elected government, nor are we likely to have one, so I address you with no greater authority than that with which liberty itself always speaks. I declare the global social space we are building to be naturally independent of the tyrannies you seek to impose on us. You have no moral right to rule us nor do you possess any methods of enforcement we have true reason to fear.

Governments derive their just powers from the consent of the governed. You have neither solicited nor received ours. We did not invite you. You do not know us, nor do you know our world. Cyberspace does not lie within your borders. Do not think that you can build it, as though it were a public construction project. You cannot. It is an act of nature and it grows itself through our collective actions.

You have not engaged in our great and gathering conversation, nor did you create the wealth of our marketplaces. You do not know our culture, our ethics, or the unwritten codes that already provide our society more order than could be obtained by any of your impositions.

You claim there are problems among us that you need to solve. You use this claim as an excuse to invade our precincts. Many of these problems don't exist. Where there are real conflicts, where there are wrongs, we will identify them and address them by our means. We are forming our own Social Contract. This governance will arise according to the conditions of our world, not yours. Our world is different.

Cyberspace consists of transactions, relationships, and thought itself, arrayed like a standing wave in the web of our communications. Ours is a world that is both everywhere and nowhere, but it is not where bodies live.

(John Perry Barlow, *A Declaration of the Independence of Cyberspace*, 1996)

THE CARTOGRAPHIC ATTRIBUTES OF THE INVISIBLE[1]

The internet used to be a faraway place. You would tap into the net through a clunky terminal and be transported into another world. People talked about travelling down an information superhighway, and surfing the net. We would enter a cyberspace and get 'online'. It was never fully clear where the internet was, but what all of those visions had in common is that they weren't *here*. John Perry Barlow's 'Declaration of the Independence of Cyberspace' famously summed up some of these transcendent visions. The internet was a new world for all of us to build: a world with its own culture, economy, politics, ethics and – most importantly – space.

But with every year since the penning of that Declaration in the late 1990s, something else has happened instead. We have found ever more ways of embedding the internet into everyday life and everyday places.

Temperance Street, Manchester

Temperance Street in Manchester is a short road that is only a stone's throw from Manchester Piccadilly train station. It looks a lot like many other streets near British railway stations: on one side there is a brick viaduct for the main rail line into Piccadilly. The arches under the viaduct host garages, wholesalers and other businesses that don't necessarily need to be in a more trafficked area. Moss, weeds and bushes grow out of the bricks, giving the road a relatively unkempt – even dishevelled – look.

Temperance Street is therefore a rather unassuming place, and most people from outside of Manchester (and indeed many within it) had likely never heard of it until Google Street View helped to bring this small corner of the city to fame. However, the attention it received was not necessarily the sort of attention that the Manchester tourist board would have chosen.

---

1. This phrase was coined by William Gibson in his 2008 novel, *Spook Country*.

Like most European cities, most of Manchester is mapped by Google's Street View feature, which allows people to virtually 'be there' in a three-dimensional snapshot of every navigable part of the city. Ironically, Temperance Street – named after the nineteenth-century mass movement to promote abstinence from excesses – was the site of an extremely public sex act. Anyone using Google Maps to navigate through that part of the city to the station wouldn't just see the garages, parked cars and railway arches that make up Temperance Street; they would also see an image of a woman performing fellatio on a man leaning, pants down, against the viaduct.

After being noticed, the image quickly went viral. Journalists expressed shock that such a scene could be found in Google's depiction of Manchester, and social media commentators took great delight in seeing the city documented in such a raw and uncensored way. Before long, Google had removed the offending stretch of road from Street View.

Where is Jerusalem?

The city of Jerusalem has been at the centre of ethno-political struggles for millennia. As a holy city to Jews, Christians and Muslims, the city is ascribed with tremendous importance by adherents of all of those faiths. The western neighbourhoods of the city are primarily home to Jewish residents and have been under Israeli rule since the 1948 Arab–Israeli War. East Jerusalem, on the other hand, is home to almost all of the city's Muslim population, although Israel has administered East Jerusalem since 1967 – that is, following the Six-Day War. The city serves as the capital of the Israeli state, while also being the desired location for the capital of the State of Palestine. However, most of the rest of the world refuses to recognise the city as the capital of either state: which is why it was such a newsworthy event when the US Embassy was moved from Tel Aviv to Jerusalem in May 2018, following a campaign promise made by Donald Trump the previous year. These fundamentally differing – and apparently irreconcilable – views about the status of this contested city in many ways lie at the very heart of the Israeli–Palestinian conflict.

Of course, a key way that many people learn about the city is through Wikipedia. Indeed, every major Western search engine links to Wikipedia's Jerusalem article when conducting a search for the city. Jerusalem is one of the encyclopaedia's most popular pages, and – because of Wikipedia's open licence – content on the Jerusalem page ends up being reused and replicated elsewhere on the internet, from Facebook to weather apps. As such, it should come as no surprise that the page itself is highly susceptible to editorial conflict.

One of the many ways in which this conflict has been manifested is through the question of how best to represent its capital city status. At the time of writing in early summer 2021, the English version of Wikipedia (after much battling between various editors) notes in the first paragraph of the article that 'Both Israel and the Palestinian Authority claim Jerusalem as their capital, as Israel maintains its primary governmental institutions there and the State of Palestine ultimately foresees it as its seat of power; however, neither claim is widely recognized internationally.' This contrasts noticeably with the Arabic Wikipedia's opening claim that Jerusalem is 'the largest city in occupied Palestine' and the Hebrew Wikipedia's opening sentence that 'Jerusalem is the capital city of the State of Israel.' In this peer-produced encyclopaedia that – famously – anyone can edit, we see different people and communities wanting to represent the exact same place in fundamentally divergent ways.

The West African Ebola epidemic

In early 2014, the West African country of Guinea faced an early outbreak of Ebola, now widely known as one of the world's deadliest diseases with an average fatality rate of 50 per cent. At the time there were no vaccines or treatments for Ebola available, beyond supportive care with rehydration and symptomatic treatment. After its initial reporting in rural Guinea, it subsequently spread to the densely populated capital Conakry, then to neighbouring Liberia and Sierra Leone and beyond. Global aid organisations such as Médecins Sans Frontières and the Red Cross were ready to spring into action with medical aid, but quickly found that large parts of the affected regions were as yet unmapped in commercial or public sources. In order to coordinate aid, their field logistics teams needed population estimates to prepare sufficient provisions, and they needed information about the local road network to coordinate delivery. Instead, they were faced with a blank map – neither the national mapping agencies nor commercial geodata providers had mapped the affected areas (Clark 2014).

This geospatial information gap was ultimately resolved by an unusual collaborator: the Humanitarian OpenStreetMap Team (HOT), a global non-profit organisation that specialises in the production of crowdsourced digital maps, traced from satellite imagery by a global volunteer force, with the specific intention to support humanitarian aid. In response, HOT organisers initiated a multi-month effort to recruit and train digital volunteers at large scale, resulting in its largest mapping project to date. Ultimately the effort was successful, and new map data were quickly made available to coordinators, drastically improving the capacity of aid organisations to provide medical support (Clark 2014; Dawson 2014).

These volunteer maps can have significant reach beyond their primary purpose. Thanks to OpenStreetMaps' open licence, other mapping providers are able to integrate these volunteer contributions into their own maps. For example, both Google Maps and Bing maps are now selectively integrating OpenStreetMap data into their own maps of remote areas in order to fill in coverage gaps. As a consequence, volunteer maps that have been collected in the context of disaster response become significant digital representations of places that have fewer alternatives available, commercial or public. In a sense, we can consider these initiatives as part of an effort to improve digital representation of the Global South, even if that is not necessarily the primary aim of the original work.

And yet, we can also consider them to be 'outsider maps' – both in the sense of being volunteer efforts by non-professional and professional cartographers alike, but also remote efforts by people from outside the areas they are representing. The maps are typically traced from satellite imagery by remote mappers who lack local knowledge of the terrain and the street-level experience of the places they map. Thematically, disaster-response maps focus on a limited set of functional concerns that are needed for field logistics, such as road networks to plan transport routes, and the tracing of settlements to support population estimates. The resulting representations are insufficient to navigate a city, at least not without first having to augment them with further information such as street names and the locations of public amenities.

What are digital geographies, and why do they matter?

The three cases presented here range from the humorous to the life changing, but what they have in common is that they tell us stories about how digital information is enrolled into everyday geographies. When most people think about geography, they tend to think about the study of the world's mountains, rivers and place names. Yet, it's guaranteed that if you approach a professional geographer with the joke that their job involves memorising the name of all the world's capital cities, you'll be met with an eye roll.

Geography is location. It is interconnections, flows and networks. It is both materiality and discourse. It is grounded, but in flux. It has a multiplicity of histories and futures. It is local, global and relational. It is space and time. It is undergoing continual augmentation by the anthroposphere. It is made up of memory and imagination. It is a platform and a process. It both shapes and is shaped by geometries of power. It is experienced, produced and continuously brought into being. And, it is, of course, also digital.

At the end of the day, we care about geography because we care about the world: the environmental, economic, social and political contexts, ecosystems and networks that we are embedded in. We care about how things work, how things are represented and the relationships between those things. So, think about the place that you live in. There are surely some local conflicts about land ownership; about who gets to have a say in how, where and for whom new buildings are built. There are also likely conflicts about how things are represented: perhaps whether a street should be renamed to avoid commemorating that historical figure who now looks somewhat less heroic and noble than he used to.

In the digital age, some of these concerns merge. By augmenting our world with digital information, contemporary information technologies shape both the ways in which geographies are structured and the ways in which they are represented. Indeed, it starts to become hard to distinguish between those things.

As the digital is ever more infused into our everyday lives, John Perry Barlow's vision of what the internet was, and could be, is revealed as simple wishful thinking. The geography of the internet no longer involves just a mapping of virtual realities and digital worlds. Indeed, the examples above show that the cities we live in are much more than just their material presences. Take the place that you live in as an example: you're surrounded by buildings and roads, concrete, bricks and glass, houses and shops. But you're also surrounded by information and code that is invisible to the naked eye but which fundamentally alters how the city functions and how we interact with it.

What this means is that we are *all* now digital geographers. The cities that we live in are shaped by a digital bedrock, by palimpsests of digital infrastructure and architecture, and by the digital mediums and platforms that support much of our social relations.

We use the term 'palimpsest' here not in the way that a historian or librarian would use the term. For them, a palimpsest is a page, typically of expensive but durable vellum, that has been recycled and reused (see Figure 1.1 for a palimpsest containing parts of the Gospel of St Luke, as well as portions of the treatise by Severus of Antioch against John the Grammarian, Homer's *Iliad* and Euclid's *Elements*). Because the earlier writings could never be fully erased despite repeated scraping, every writing block was a composite containing the superimposed traces of all previous texts (Crang 1996). This sort of layering, in which today's surface is built over – and part of – the many that came before, can be used as a neat analogy for the contemporary city (Graham 2018). The city, in other words, is a palimpsest of material and digital strata that are interwoven and interlayered. Digital layers, together with material layers, compound over time.

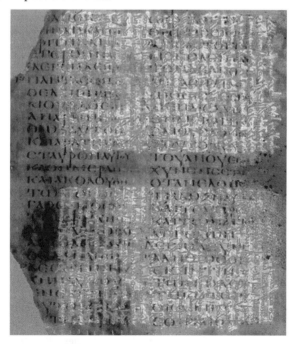

Figure 1.1   The Codex Nitriensis. A Greek and Syriac palimpsest formerly belonging to the monastery of St Mary Deipara in the Nitrian Desert, northern Egypt, and now held by the British Museum. Source: Wikimedia Commons.

FROM COSMOGRAPHIES TO DIGITAL GEOGRAPHIES

As we have discussed, our use of 'digital geographies' takes 'digital' to include technologies and the artifacts they produce, but also the practices and discourses surrounding them. So, in other words, we are talking about the ways in which such information surrounds and envelops our everyday lives.

If we think of those technologies, artifacts, practices and discourses as all having geographies, it is useful to think about them in three primary ways, following Ash et al. (2016). These are geographies *of* the digital (e.g. the geography of digital information), geographies *produced by* the digital (e.g. the mediation of everyday life through digital mechanisms), and geographies *produced through* the digital (e.g. geography captured through digital mechanisms). For the purposes of our mission in this book, we deploy a somewhat narrower operationalisation of the term. We will mainly use 'digital geography' as a shorthand for geographies of the digital (such as digital geospatial information). This book therefore will focus on two of today's most important sites of maps and geographic information – Google and Wikipedia – and the representations they create of the world. However, in doing so, we will also be able to make inferences about geographies *produced by* the digital.

To do any of this, we need to make sure we properly understand the cartographic attributes of the invisible. We need to make sure that we're able to map, measure and critically interrogate digital geographies.

In this book we seek to understand where digital geographies come from, what they depict (and leave out), and what happens when they are contested. We will ask how digital geographies exert power, who exerts power within them, where it is exerted and who it is exerted for and against, the mechanisms through which it is exerted, and ultimately how can we design more equitable alternatives. We do this through case studies of two of the world's most important digital platforms: Google and Wikipedia. But to explain why we focus on those two platforms in particular, we'd like to first take you back to the work that was being produced hundreds of years ago in the form of so-called 'cosmographies'.

Early cosmographers set themselves the modest task of collating all knowledge about the world or universe, captured and represented as ordered collections of universal truths.[2] While cosmographers were invested with considerable amounts of freedom to interpret the universe in whatever ways they saw fit, the universal knowledge presented by the many late Renaissance and early Enlightenment cosmographers was obviously coloured and shaped by the dominant social and political forces at the time.

An example is William Cunningham's 1559 cosmography entitled *The Cosmographical Glasse*, a collection of information about world regions, human races, climate, biology, zoology and religious and cultural behaviour. But it was also overtly shaped by Cunningham's personal beliefs, notably the ways in which he described every region of the world as being governed by particular astrological laws (Livingstone 1992). Similarly, the Franciscan friar Vincenzo Coronelli 'sought to bring the ends of the earth within the scope of a single illustrated text' (Cosgrove 1999, p. 41). One of his most noted projects was the construction of two giant globes which were supposed to be empirically accurate representations of reality. And yet, at the same time, the content of globes was highly influenced by their patron Louis XIV, the Sun King, so much so that the stars are fixed in the location at which they were to be found at the birth of the king.

So while myriad instances of cosmographic knowledge existed, each proclaimed to reveal universal truth. This inherent contradiction in the nature of cosmographic knowledge was likely a factor in the formation of a new way of understanding the universe: natural history. The knowledge-building project of natural history was intended to observe and catalogue nature in order to construct a 'planetary consciousness' (Pratt 1992), which itself was part of a larger enlightenment ontology which sought to understand and catalogue truth using objective scientific methods.

This can be seen in the mid-eighteenth-century work of Carl Linné who developed a descriptive system that could be used to classify all known and unknown plants on the Earth into one of 24 categories. The periodic table of elements, developed later in the nineteenth century, similarly classifies and arranges chemical elements in terms of their characteristics. Systems like these ordered chaos in a predetermined way,

---

2. The Greek word 'Kosmos' describes order and harmonious arrangement – a cosmography is therefore an ordered mapping or understanding of how the universe is arranged and works.

and the rules of the ordering were to be systematically established by a few European scientists.

This ambitious project of systemising global knowledge had never before been attempted. Reality was no longer open to subjective interpretation. In a highly reductionist manner, everything in the universe could be described in predetermined ways and placed into predetermined systems. Once the grid was constructed, 'every visible square, or even cubic, inch of the earth's surface' (Pratt 1992, p. 30) would fall into its unquestionable place within it. The planetary consciousness this system gave rise to was both pervasive and imperial. It extended to all corners of the globe and did not tolerate alternate epistemologies. Local and individual epistemologies were now irrelevant to the established system. Local knowledge could only contribute to the scientific project insofar as it could be moulded into the scientific system. And while this meant that knowledge was often pushed, crammed and twisted into its proper place in the classificatory system, the dominant epistemological grids, established in European centres, both structured the nature of the universe and established the meaning of truth.

Practices of knowledge production have moved on significantly in the digital age. There are active efforts to decentre systems of knowledge and to invite a multitude of voices from the margins. However, what hasn't changed is the totalising, cosmographical ambition. Today, Google and Wikipedia are two of the largest publicly available platforms that aggregate geographic knowledge. From Wikipedia's original mission to be 'the sum of all human knowledge' to Google's to 'organise all the world's information', both platforms have cosmographical ambitions.

The 'mission' and 'purpose' statements of both platforms at the time of writing are no less universal in their objectives. Google Maps proudly boasts of its ability to represent *everywhere*: 'What is a map when it's more than just a map? It's a tour of the moon, a ticket to Mars, and a bird's-eye view of Earth, from the highest mountains to the lowest valleys and everywhere in between.' Wikipedia is no less ambitious in claiming that it 'has a lofty goal: a comprehensive collection of all of the knowledge in the world [...] Wikipedia is intended to be the largest, most comprehensive, and most widely-available encyclopedia ever written.'

These two platforms don't just matter because of their grand ambitions, but also because together they mediate a significant amount of information for the world's internet users. Content from Wikipedia is used in Google's Knowledge Graph that appears on the first page of search results. If a user searches for a name for example, Google displays biographical data from Wikipedia. Google is the world's most popular search engine in almost every country in the world (with only Russia and China[3,4] as large and notable exceptions).

MAPS ARE NOT THE TERRITORY

The first thing most people notice when looking at a historical map is just how inaccurate it is. We don't just mean the fantastical creatures and monsters that can be found in some pre-modern maps (Figure 1.2), or the glib labels of 'terra incognita' or 'mare incognitum' placed over unexplored parts of the globe, but simply the more subtle distortions, omissions and embellishments that we aren't accustomed to seeing on contemporary maps. That is because the cartographic technologies that underpin the maps we use today leave little to the imagination. We no longer wonder if there is land west of Europe, whether California is an island, and if there really be dragons in the far north. Today's maps are much more objective – indeed, accurate and truthful – representations of the world, right?

The answer is 'not really'. Of course, we don't mean to imply that the dragons and strange sea creatures of the Carta Marina have any place in today's cartographic projects. However, it is important to remember that while today's maps may seem accurate, precise and objective, there is no such thing as a true or complete map. Every map is (necessarily) a selective representation of the world, and in taming and making sense of the world's infinite complexity, every map has its own particular and subjective story to tell.

Street maps take much care in distinguishing between different types of road, but tell you little about the presence or absence of potholes. Topographic maps give us a rich sense of the contours of the landscape, offering clues for how to navigate it physically, but reveal little about the

---

3. The most popular search engines in Russia and China are Yandex and Baidu respectively. In 2010 Google shut down their search engine in China and has not since resumed operations.

4. As we discuss in Chapter 4, Chinese citizens are the world's largest digitally connected population but Google and Wikipedia are not widely used in China. Internet geographies in China therefore fall out of focus in our research and there are many points in the book in which 'What about China?' would be a perfectly valid question to ask. We acknowledge this blind-spot, and acknowledge that we don't have good answers to the aforementioned question.

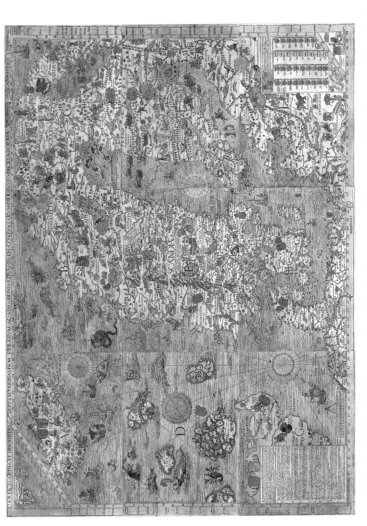

Figure 1.2 The Carta Marina. This 'carta marina et descriptio septentrionalium terrarum' (Marine map and description of the Northern lands) was created by Olaus Magnus in Rome in 1527–39. Drawing on a number of sources, it was the first map of the Nordic countries to give details and place names. Source: Wikimedia Commons.

local economy or (for example) where to get a drink having done so. And political maps reveal a lot about who governs the world, and yet they aren't much use for navigation. Maps must always tell selective stories if they are to be legible at all, and if they are to effectively address the purposes of their design (Monmonier 1996). These selective stories are necessitated by the physical limitations of their medium[5] (not everything can be shown) and the purposes for which they were designed (omission, emphasis, simplification and distortion are necessary in every map). Restrictions may differ for digital maps, but they still exist.

The issue, then, is that showing what and who exists (and who doesn't), who owns land and who doesn't, where you should go and where you shouldn't, is always a design choice imbued with power and politics. Maps matter because they are able to inscribe identities by fixing and ordering lines, distinctions and hierarchies, and in so doing stabilising one out of many potential meanings. Where there is contestation, they need to take a stance, pick a side. They cannot remain on the sidelines. Indeed, they are much more than just lines on paper, they are ways of telling stories in a way that exerts power, because there will always be silenced voices and lines left undrawn (Pickles 2004).

We see this in the ways that maps have always allowed those with power to claim 'this is mine; these are the boundaries' (Harley 1989). They take a messy world full of complicated relationships and give it a fixed, bounded and simplified form. We see these contours of representational control enacted at every scale of human activity: from gendered household practices (Moss and Al-Hindi 2007) to political interactions between countries. During the colonial era, for instance, it was commonplace for Western maps to faithfully record straight lines drawn across Native American, Asian and African territories (Winichakul 1994). Those lines bore little relation to lived experiences on the ground. This could be done to reinforce what Spivak (1985) describes as the 'necessary yet contradictory assumptions of an uninscribed earth' – the idea that nothing was *there* before the coloniser. Cartographers – and those who govern the map – manufacture power, and maps inherently have politics.

Particular spatial knowledges have not just been used to explicitly claim dominion over the world, but also to enforce more insidious and

---

5.   Projection choice is one of the oldest examples of this. Maps have had to use projections to depict parts, or all, of the Earth's three-dimensional sphere onto a two-dimensional surface. Every map projection therefore necessarily distorts some combination of area, direction, shape, bearing and distance.

duplicitous representations of the world's economic peripheries. Edward Saïd (1978), and many since him, have indicated how orientalised representations of the world are not simply produced and reproduced by those who occupy positions of privilege in the global network of knowledge; these representations are also internalised in the discourses coming from the peripheries. Compounding the subordination (and sometimes outright erasure) of local voice is the digital mediation of spatial knowledges enabled by GIS-based maps,[6] which in presenting a view from above erase both the positionality of the user and the social contexts under which those knowledges are produced (Elwood 2006; Goss 1995; Roberts and Schein 1995). Many technologies and techno-mediated platforms designed in and for Western contexts are grounded in an enlightenment perspective that truth itself is the 'view from nowhere' (Nagel 1986). But, of course, we know this not to be the case, as even the most dominant knowledges and truths must emerge from a particular place (Shapin 1998).

Without giving a full account of the historical geographies of spatial knowledges,[7] it should suffice to point out that centralisation and control of knowledge production is nothing new, and that this centralisation has served the world's economic cores well. Bruno Latour (1986) has argued that 'the foundation of European science lies in the massive accumulation of basic knowledge of the world made possible by Europe's central position in a system of colonial empires – a place where knowledge and resources were brought from around the world' (Takhteyev 2012, p. 43).

Our aim here has to begin by highlighting how maps and other representations of place are subject to measurement constraints, and how their creation involves a large number of design choices, which frequently lead to distortions, misrepresentations and manipulation (see Livingstone 1992; Pickles 2004). As a consequence, maps are far from objective representations of the world. They are shaped both by complex layers of history and meaning, including the judgements of the mapmaker, and by a technical and often rigid vocabulary of quantified and spatially referenced geometries. Scholars such as Harley (1989) have argued that maps are not 'the territory', but are 'rather technologies which normalize, legitimate, underwrite, and render transparent

---

6.   GIS map technology allows for the layering of different kinds of data onto a geographical point.

7.   A number of authors have given the topic a thorough treatment, including Livingstone (1992).

material exercises of power' (Ash et al. 2016). Harley's assertion that maps are not the territory is made to stress the fact that maps are not objective representations of the world; that there are no, and never have been, neutral maps. But our next chapter will question that premise, and ask whether our digital moment is leading maps to become the territory. Digital maps, rather than reproducing the God's-eye view, often place the viewer within the representation itself.

The entire reason why the lines on a map matter is because maps do more than depict the world. They change the world. They impact how we interact with the world and understand the world. In doing so, they shape the world itself. The book focuses on Google and Wikipedia as those platforms, with their cosmographical ambitions, play an outsized role in both representing and reshaping today's world. We will use them as sites to ask questions about what is, and isn't, digitally represented; who does, and doesn't, get to participate in those representations; and who the winners and losers are when we don't all agree. As these digital tools increasingly shape how we understand, navigate and ultimately produce the world, our aim is to map the mappers, and ask what sort of world they are creating.

2

When the Map Becomes the Territory[1]

> To catalogue the world is to appropriate it.
>
> (Barthes 1980, p. 27)

Information has always had geography. It is from somewhere; about somewhere; it evolves and is transformed somewhere; it is mediated by networks, infrastructures and technologies: all of which exist in physical, material places. Information has also always been mobile. Even one of the most commonly used definitions of information – 'the imparting of knowledge in general' (*Oxford English Dictionary* 2015) – emphasises the transmission and movement of information in an ongoing and dynamic process. In short, information – ranging from standardised measurements to instruction manuals to stories and news – emerges from, engages with, and is adapted to a range of local contexts and geographies (Elwood and Leszczynski 2013).

It is the mobility and adaptability of information that provides the motivation to constrain its mutability through the creation of what Bruno Latour (1986) refers to as 'immutable mobiles': that is, information that can be transported without significant change to its inherent characteristics or meaning. The printing press, for instance, made it relatively cheap to create and transport information through the medium of printed paper while simultaneously limiting how its form could change subsequently. As digital-enabled, non-proximate communication emerged and was adopted by governments and companies, the ability to create 'immutable mobiles' – that is, shared understandings of information by populations in different locations across time – became vital. Information and power thus became intimately intertwined as people capitalised on the value associated with epistemic control: information represented 'this' and

---

1.   Some of the text in this chapter is a reworking of the following article: Graham, M., S. De Sabbata and M. Zook. 2015. 'Towards a Study of Information Geographies: (Im)mutable Augmentations and a Mapping of the Geographies of Information'. *Geo: Geography and Environment* 2(1): 88–105. doi:10.1002/geo2.8.

not 'that', and there was power in telling people as much (Foucault 2000; Schech 2002).

Geographical knowledge has been implicated in this dynamic. A key characteristic of immutable mobiles is their ability to crystallise informational layers of places in a 'moveable container'; to create particular 'geographies of information' (Wilson 2017). A map, a tourist guide or a postcard all annotate a bounded part of the world in a relatively immutable form (printed paper) that can be physically moved around the world. Thus, immutable mobiles shape how places are used, understood and engaged with (Dodge and Kitchin 2007; Kitchin 2011). By abstracting information about place and capturing it in the (relatively) immutable form of printed paper, we simultaneously fix information to a physical object, and untether it from place. In the era of print, the geography of immutable mobiles such as maps or books largely defined the geography of codified and geographically referenced information.

Today, digital technologies have facilitated an evolution of information beyond immutable mobiles through the creation of '(im)mutable augmentations', characterised by the layering of dynamic information over and across geographic space. Thus, not only does information have particular geographies, but geography itself is layered, defined and augmented by information that is more or less immutable, depending upon the institutions and practices associated with it (Perkins 2014). The Sydney Opera House, for instance, is not just a building made from bricks and mortar. Nor is it simply represented by guidebook entries, postcards and other immutable mobiles that are fixed in printed paper. It is also overlaid with digital images, videos, descriptions, reviews about tours and past performances, as well as innumerable stories told about experiences associated with it that are stored and organised in online maps and websites. All of those things are informational, but they are also part of the place itself – that is, they are part of how we enact and bring the place into being (Graham, Zook and Boulton 2013; Leszczynski 2015). The advent of the (im)mutable augmentations and mobile tools that allow us to access this information while in situ – for shopping, wayfinding, driving, sightseeing, protesting and many other geographically constrained activities – places an ever-greater value in the epistemic control to fix informational layers of place (Graham, Zook and Boulton 2013). In theory, everyone can access and *contribute* digitally to this map of knowledge. The question then arises: who controls how and what places are represented and understood?

These (im)mutable augmentations of information about places matter because they shape how we are able to find and understand different parts of the world (Shelton et al. 2014). Places that are invisible or excluded from geographic representations will be equally invisible in practice to many people. A restaurant omitted from a map can cease to be a restaurant if nobody finds it, or knows it exists. Likewise, how places are presented within informational augmentations fundamentally affects how they are used or brought into being (Graham and Zook 2013). In other words, geographic augmentations are much more than just representations of places: they are part of the place itself; they shape it rather than simply reflect it; and the map again becomes part of the territory (Pickles 2004; Leszczynski 2015). The logical conclusion is that annotations of place can emerge as important sites of political contestation: with different groups of people trying to impose different narratives on informational augmentations (Zook and Graham 2007). Should the city in Northern Ireland be labelled as Derry or Londonderry? Is it the Falklands or Las Malvinas? And which country is Crimea in?[2]

Digital information, then, has become part of the spaces that we live in. But what exactly do we mean by 'space' in the first place? We approach this topic through a relational understanding of space (e.g. Lefebvre 1991). What we mean here is that space is not fixed, nor is it a container for the lived experiences that happen on its surface. Instead, and following Doreen Massey (2005), we define space as being both constituted through interrelated social relations, and always in a state of becoming; always under construction. Space, in other words, is neither predetermined, predefined or natural (Dodge and Kitchin 2005). It is instead only ever what we make of it.

Geography is therefore something we bring into being; and, increasingly we bring it into being through digital tools, technologies, algorithms and data. These observations are not particularly new. Over 20 years ago, Stephen Graham (1998) envisioned recombinatory and relational interactions between cities, space and information. He has since pointed to what he refers to as software-sorted geographies: landscapes that are often shaped, formed and mediated by invisible lines of code (see e.g. Graham 2005). Martin Dodge and Rob Kitchin (2005) have emphasised 'code/space': the ways that space is brought into being with digital code

---

2. Here we refer to historically and politically disputed territories in the last century. For further detail on each territory, see Brunet-Jailly (2015).

as a key factor in placemaking. They illustrate that the 'technicity' of code (its power to bring about action) is able to influence our spatial experiences and actions through processes of transduction (constant remaking and re-enactions).

Our aim in this book is to further argue that the digital age, by facilitating (im)mutable augmentations, has given platforms like Google and Wikipedia a crucial role in determining how space is constructed, and how we perceive it as users of their services. As the map becomes the territory, the mappers play an important role in shaping what space becomes.

PRE-DIGITAL GEOGRAPHIES OF INFORMATION

In the pre-digital age, the affordances of technologies and associated socio-technical systems for collecting, storing and disseminating information meant that information was both scarce and geographically embedded. For instance, at the dawn of the nineteenth century the tools for collating encyclopaedic information about places (e.g. compasses, paper, sextants) were concentrated in only a few hands and places; making the ability to engage in large-scale data collection relatively rare. Even more so, because the required propinquity to the object of measurement inherent in collecting information about places entailed a scale of organisation not widely available. Likewise, the state of the art for containing information – the book – required specific points of access to codified content for its production. Books were also constrained by a particular form – two-dimensional printed material of pre-specified dimensions, typically part of a linear reading trajectory from start to finish – and method of physical storage in particular places.

Other key bottlenecks in the processing of information have included the availability of necessary skill sets to manage, validate, merge, modify, classify, sort, analyse and manipulate information into particular forms and formats. The institutions that emerged to meet this challenge – universities, associations and guilds – required resources (which, in turn, often needed to be 'spatially fixed') and, as a result, formalised education in information handling practices was necessarily place-bound and concentrated in specific places. These geographic centres of calculation meant that the ability to access codified information, let alone contribute to it (i.e. the professionalisation of knowledge work) was also highly constrained.

Although the affordances of pre-digital technologies (and their associated systems of governance, economisation and socialisation) allowed for movements of codified information, it could never transcend the innate materiality of its medium or the world. In short, the frictions of mobility associated with transmitting and storing information, the place-bound rules and forms of governance, and the availability of requisite technologies have all shaped the geographies of information in this era. In practice, these constraints manifest into hegemonic representations and hegemonic modes of participation (see e.g. Gramsci 1971), and because knowledge and codified information are always produced under conditions of power (Pickles 1995; Crampton 2008), control over hegemonic representations has been a way of exerting economic, social and political power (Laclau and Mouffe 1985).

In the last few centuries, books, newspapers and patents, for instance, were all far more likely to be published from (and about) the Global North, with the Global South playing a relatively minor role in producing, using and controlling codified information (Thompson and Fox-Kean 2005; M. Graham, Hale and Stephens 2011). This information power and power over information manifests into distinct spatial patterns, and almost all traditional mediums of information are characterised by significant spatial inequalities, leading Castells (1999, p. 3) to conclude that 'most of Africa is being left in a technological apartheid'. Castells (2010) goes on to characterise the systemic and uneven relationship between information production/use and socio-economic exclusion and marginalisation as the 'black holes of informational capitalism'.

DEMOCRATISING GEOGRAPHIES AND ECONOMIES?

So far, we have a story in which most maps of power have been elite objects: containing inputs from relatively few people and controlled by even fewer (see also Elwood and Leszczynski 2013). But, against this backdrop, recent decades have seen a sea change in the availability of information. The terms 'information revolution' (Floridi 2014) and 'data revolution' (Kitchin 2014) signify the radical changes in the ways that information is produced and used: implying that we no longer live in an age of information scarcity. This transformation has been brought about by the proliferation of new socio-technical systems of the so-called digital age. These systems are underpinned by greater accessibility to computers that can readily receive, process and transmit information non-proximally, as well as a host of associated social, economic and political practices. As a result, many of the economic barriers to the production, processing and proliferation of information in the pre-digital era have been drastically lowered.

Some have argued that this emerging digital age offers a potentially radically different political economy of information (Benkler 2006; Jenkins 2006; Bruns 2008). Tapscott and Williams (2006) and Shirky (2011) highlight the ways that digitally mediated participation and representation is broad-based, circumventing traditional mediators of information, and allowing citizens to play a more significant role in shaping the content and augmentations that play key roles in their lives (see also Sui and Goodchild 2011). Harvard law professor Lawrence Lessig, a key scholar of the effects of information systems on property rights, has also made some particularly hopeful observations on the democratic power of the internet. At the 2003 World Summit on the Information Society, he pointed to the significant possibilities afforded by the Web: '[f]or the first time in a millennium, we have a technology to equalize the opportunity that people have to access and participate in the construction of knowledge and culture, regardless of their geographic placing' (Lessig 2003). Lessig's characterisation is not unique; such sentiments also infuse the world of policy and business. In 2012 the Secretary-General of the International Telecommunication Union claimed that once internet connectivity arrives, 'all the world's citizens will have the potential to access unlimited knowledge, to express themselves freely, and to contribute to and enjoy the benefits of the knowledge society' (Touré 2012). Echoing a similar line of positive aspiration, Wikipedia seeks to 'contain the sum of all human knowledge', and Google's stated core mission is to 'organize the world's information and make it universally accessible and useful' (Google 2020).

These are powerful statements, and they permeate all levels of discourse about digital technologies and development. While we are disposed to be suspicious of such totalising claims, to date, the existing work on global geographies of information (see Zook 2001; Malecki 2002; Devriendt et al. 2011) has tended to use (similar) single indicators rather than a comparison of a range of variables to more completely capture the bigger picture associated with the changing political economy of information. To be sure, the macro-picture is one of extreme connectivity – now that more than half the global population is connected to the internet there are more mobile phones than people, and billions of devices are attached to the global network – but how has this altered the political economy and geography of information?[3] Has this proliferation of access altered participation or representation? Are the changing socio-technical systems identified by scholars, policy-makers and corporations, changing information geographies? In other words, because people can, in theory, create and access information about and from almost anywhere on Earth, are we indeed seeing different geographies of participation and representation, or new layers of digital augmentations (i.e. data shadows; Graham 2010), that are associated with places?

Not only has the ability to create digital information been opened up, so too has the ability to publish and disseminate it. Commons-based platforms, especially Wikipedia, have proved that the entire process of production and dissemination can be opened up. As the following chapter will show, now anyone can be a mapper.

---

3. See Agnieszka Leszczynski's (2012) 'Situating the Geoweb in Political Economy' for a review on this topic.

3
Making Digital Geographies

So far, we have argued that digital information is an integral part of contemporary places. It both represents the world and forms part of it. Two platforms, Google and Wikipedia, host many of our interactions with such digital information – we discussed their importance in the opening chapter. Those platforms are therefore two of the world's most important map-makers.

As part of our investigation in this chapter and throughout the book we will ask questions about the broader information ecologies within which this contemporary map-making activity takes place, and discuss key barriers to global participation and representation. But in order to be able to interpret what goes into digital descriptions and augmentations of place, and to think about the ways that they matter to everyday life, we first need to dig deeper into their provenance. This chapter lifts the lid on the two globe-spanning platforms that form the object of this book's inquiry, asking who and what is involved in the process of their creation. Where does that information come from? How is it gathered, organised, controlled, contested and displayed?

This chapter peers behind our screens to shed light on the modes of production and the systems of control used to generate, structure and create the constituent parts of our digital *umwelt*. Specifically, we ask where platforms like Google and Wikipedia get their underpinning digital information from, and how that information is governed and processed. Doing so allows us to understand how the foundational features of both platforms influence how they represent the world.

The chapter is organised into four major sections, corresponding to four foundational concerns:

1. Data collection – how is the digital information created?
2. Organisation and control – how is the vast universe of digital information organised and managed?

3. Geospatial platform ecologies – what are the emerging relationships between commercial and non-profit actors within the value chain of digital information?

4. Two complementary ontologies – to what extent do these processes and relationships shape how the world is described by these platforms?

Despite the similarity in intent between Wikipedia and Google and the cosmographies of the past – that is, an ordered and all-encompassing description of the world – the platforms are built upon fundamentally different epistemological foundations. This chapter will explain how Google is a highly centralised organisation that nevertheless produces heterogeneous representations of the world, whilst Wikipedia is a relatively decentralised organisation that produces extremely centralised representations.

THE COLLECTION OF GEOSPATIAL DATA

From data licensing to data collection

Google Maps is a fascinating case study for illustrating the institutional and industrial processes behind digital maps. It is of course a product of the collective knowledge and expertise of the many experts employed by Google, but also of novel forms of labour that are more hidden. As we will see, the processes that produce the Google Maps we use every day to navigate our world involve the integration of heterogeneous data from many sources, and are increasingly automated.

Taken together, all these elements yield a remarkable product: Google Maps is arguably the most detailed map of the world that has ever existed. The service combines street maps, satellite maps, street view images and user-generated content.

Madrigal (2012) argues that Google regards maps as infrastructures of central strategic importance: the company wants to organise the world's information whether it be digital documents or material landscapes. This is the next step in search technology – not just indexing the Web, but indexing the world. As a consequence, Google is putting immense efforts behind the creation of its digital map. In its early days in the mid-2000s, Google Maps licensed its data from well-established producers of digital maps such as Tele Atlas and Navteq (Garfield 2012). Over time it started producing its own maps based on geodata provided by third parties, including the TIGER road network data provided by the US Census Bureau, and similar data sets maintained by national bodies in other countries (Madrigal 2012). This process likely also relied on gazetteers, curated information directories that collect key information about places in the world such as their name, location and dimensions, some of which are derived from local government sources.

Taken together, the road networks and place names included in these data sets form the basis of any map that is used for navigation, yet they are merely a starting point. The contemporary digital maps we use today record significantly more detail that is not normally recorded in a central register, including detailed information about individual businesses, schools, bars and restaurants, and other local destinations. This includes their names and street addresses, as well as opening times, contact details, websites, photos, customer reviews, event listings and more – as well as similar information about the neighbourhoods and urban infrastructure that constitute a city. By creating an iterative loop between map user and map, they even record a temporal profile of population density in many places: telling users when places become more and less busy. The collection and curation of such highly heterogeneous information involves significant human effort.

Google declines to share specific details about their data suppliers, but certain details in its maps suggest it licenses geospatial data from data brokers and other third parties. One such data broker is the American technology company Pitney Bowes. Best known for the postage meters (franking machines) and other mailing services it developed in the 1920s, through a series of acquisitions the company has grown to become a geodata supplier to many of the world's most widely used digital platforms. It specialises in the collection and verification of neighbourhood data, and a small change in their database can affect the maps on hundreds of sites, including Google Maps (Dewey 2019).

Features like roads, and the names that represent them, usually exist as data that are structured, agreed-upon and standardised. But there are other types of places that lack any such canonical, or even agreed-upon, descriptions. Neighbourhood names in many cities are an example. The area of Dalston in east London, for instance, is a part of London that has never been an official administrative unit. As such, it lacks clear borders. But it nonetheless is an area that most Londoners recognise, and certainly a term that most residents of the area would use to describe their neighbourhood.[1] There are places all over the world just like this, vernacular geographies that represent the everyday knowing of space (Stansfeld 2019). People roughly know what they are and where they are; they know which parts of the city are in the neighbourhood and which aren't. But, in the spaces between the two, there is a lot that is open to interpretation. Those interpretations involve cultural knowledge and memory, which are less stable, but no less powerful and meaningful.

According to Ian White, founder of one of the companies acquired by Pitney Bowes in 2015, much of this data on neighbourhood names is collected by hand: 'There's no machine that can do this for you ... These are representations of unofficial, social spaces' (Dewey 2019). Instead, his company Urban Mapping hired college graduates to collect neighbourhood and place names in local blogs, home listings, city plans and other documents. However, Maponics, another acquisition (in 2016), was able to extract place names from images and text using computer vision and natural language processing technology.

Companies like Pitney Bowes collect such informally held knowledge, often involving significant manual effort, and in turn license the resulting information to commercial users of their geospatial databases. Under such licensing arrangements, the granter of a licence holds and retains exclusive legal rights to the data, which allows them to become an exclusive owner of the information – even if in principle the knowledge contained in the information is already in the public domain. Licensing terms typically place limits on the ways in which the data can be used, for example preventing the information from being resold, or requiring the granter of a licence to be credited in any works that make use of the data.

While such licensed data sets allowed Google to develop their first maps relatively quickly, the Google Maps of today is increasingly dependent on data that Google has collected itself. In some ways the data collection process for Google Maps is comparable to the use of web crawlers to feed Google's search engine: it too relies on the indexing of web content to extract information about the opening times of restaurants, and other details. In addition, however, Google has increasingly collected information in the physical world. Maybe most widely known is its Street View feature, discussed in Chapter 1 in reference to the controversy around Temperance Street in Manchester. Fleets of cars record

---

1. Like many parts of London, it originated as a village – referenced in 1294 as 'Derleston', and probably derived from 'Deorlaf's tun' or farm – which was engulfed by the rapidly expanding city, but never defined as an administrative unit with clear boundaries.

geographic traces of the road network – photographs of everything visible from the street that can be used to aid map users in their navigation, and even the locations of commercial and home WiFi networks which can be used to triangulate a phone within the city, locating it on the map it is displaying. Yet as we will see, these data points are merely a starting point for an increasingly sophisticated production chain.

Crowdsourcing, opportunist data collection and hidden human labour

Customers are another important element of the Google Maps production chain. In the early years of Google Maps, the free product Google Map Maker allowed users to propose changes to Google's maps, as a bottom-up and public-facing complement to its internal data collection processes. The product has since been discontinued, but many of its features have returned as part of the main map product (Google 2017). As part of this, Google Maps asks its users to post reviews for venues and locations shown on the map, which it rewards with virtual points and badges. It promotes the most active reviewers to Local Guide, a status that yields additional capacities to provide detailed information about places on the map, and gives access to a private community forum. Google also offers a MyBusiness portal where business owners can manage the metadata describing their business, including the capacity to upload indoor maps of their property.

Such activities can be considered forms of 'crowdsourcing', a term that was initially coined by Howe (2006) in *Wired* magazine, and has since then acquired a number of different meanings. Pedersen et al. (2013) attempt a definition of the term: 'A collaboration model enabled by people-centric web technologies to solve individual, organizational, and societal problems using a dynamically formed crowd of interested people who respond to an open call for participation.' Wiggins and Crowston (2010) add: 'Initially introduced as a novel alternative business model, more recent popular use of the term has applied it to any form of collective intelligence that draws on large numbers of participants through the internet.' Both definitions share the observation that in a crowdsourcing system, tasks are typically described by a central coordinating party which then recruits labour for their completion – evoking connotations of outsourced volunteer labour. In practice, the term is used more loosely. For example, Wikipedia is frequently referenced in crowdsourcing research, although it has no central body that recruits labour and coordinates activities.

For commercial ventures, crowdsourcing practices are now often an important foundation for novel data-driven products. For example, the local 'search-and-discovery' mobile app Foursquare incorporates a venue-rating system comparable to that used by Google Maps, to help people find places they might like nearby: 'Dozens of signals go into our venue ratings, but the most important ones are generated by our users. Our strongest signals include explicit feedback, quick tips, and verified check-ins. We also use passive location data generated by our flagship apps, Foursquare City Guide and Foursquare Swarm, as well as through our partner data, which rely on our proprietary Pilgrim technology' (Yang and Sklar 2018).

Maybe more well-known to many internet users is Captcha, a project acquired by Google in 2009. Familiar to anyone who has had to transcribe a fuzzy series of letters and numbers before accessing a service, Captcha helps platform operators determine whether a visitor to their platform is a human or an automated script, by presenting users with a challenge that is easy for humans to solve (e.g. resolving indistinct letters) but harder for machines. Where initial versions simply asked people to read numbers and letters encoded in an image, under Google's shepherdship Captcha has progressed into a sophisticated data-collection operation that uses human input to annotate the content of street view imagery, for example by distinguishing images that show buses from those that show cars or empty streets. Many internet users who answer such challenges on a regular basis might not realise that their answers feed into Google Maps and other geospatial data efforts – a clever and efficient way to get humans to verify map features, rather than relying totally on machines.

In some cases, data collection takes place silently in the background rather than through explicit manual contributions by individuals, an approach that could be considered an opportunistic or passive form of data collection. The mobile navigation service Waze, acquired by Google in 2013, was among the first to monitor the geolocation of its users in an effort to identify traffic congestion as it took place in real time. This has not always worked as intended. During the California Wildfires in 2018, Waze was reportedly directing passengers towards streets with fires as they were less congested (Mak 2018). This method has since then been adopted by Google Maps, which has extended its use further – for example, it is now displaying information about the volume of current and historic visitor flows in shops and other public venues and estimates variable navigation times change throughout the day.

Social knowledge production on Wikipedia

We can contrast these commercial efforts with the example of Wikipedia, a participatory and collaborative system of (not-for-profit) knowledge production that largely relies on the work of a global community of self-motivated volunteers.

There has been renewed interest in the concept of commons-based peer production – alternatively peer production or social production – after it was popularised by author and law professor Yochai Benkler (2002) as an alternative model of production, after the more traditional form of commercial production by firms and market economies. In contrast, peer production is characterised by information-gathering and exchange as a key activity and output, by its decentralised and networked forms of organisation, and by the absence of explicit financial compensation for contributors (Benkler 2002, p. 375). According to Benkler, this model of production can exceed the others in efficiency because knowledge of tasks and capabilities is distributed, as is the capacity to self-nominate and coordinate between participants. As a result, it allows larger groups of individuals to employ larger pools of resources towards addressing the problem at hand, and the collective effort produces a common good, or commons.

The Wikipedia contribution model constitutes maybe the largest effort of human collaboration that has ever existed – according to Geiger and Halfaker (2013) by 2012, it already represented over 100 million cumulative hours of human labour – and its participatory processes offer complementary alternatives to standard industrial structures.

Why do people contribute to Wikipedia? To an outsider it may seem counterintuitive that individuals would choose to contribute so many hours of effort towards an external cause without being paid for their labour. And yet, this degree of volunteer enthusiasm is hardly surprising: much empirical work has documented the wide range of motivations outside of financial compensation that come into play. In their model of the motivations of volunteer workers, Clary et al. (1998) distinguish six basic categories that motivate such engagement, namely: values such as altruism, the development of new and deeper understanding, social experiences around participation, career benefits, protective aspects relating to the ego such as the reduction of guilt over a perceived personal privilege, and enhancement aspects including self-improvement and attainment of a positive self-image. In a later study of Wikipedia contributor motivations, the model was augmented with two further categories: fun and ideology (2007). But another – crucially important – reason that people contribute to Wikipedia is because they believe that the content within it matters, as it is a common good. They know, in other words, that shaping Wikipedia is a way of shaping the world that it represents. Wikipedia's impact is challenging to measure and quantify, but economic studies do show clearly that presence on Wikipedia translates to increased public attention and therefore potentially, at least in the case of tourism discussed by Hinnosaar et al. (2019), higher revenues.[2] While a much more comprehensive discussion of empirically tested theories of participation in online community platforms is offered by Kraut and Resnick (2012), we can say in summary that people contribute to Wikipedia because it improves their experience of their own lives, because they enjoy doing so, because they believe it will have real-world impacts, and because they believe that the knowledge collected in Wikipedia should be free for anyone in the world to access.

Beyond these motivational aspects, a wide range of external factors contributes to Wikipedia's ongoing growth. For example, it has been observed that breaking news can lead to intense collective editing activity on particular topics (Keegan et al. 2013), and that some of the participants in such moments may be first-time editors who only make small changes. In other words, global news moments – earthquakes, plane crashes, elections – can be significant recruiting events for crowdsourcing platforms. However, this does not mean that these newcomers necessarily become long-term contributors (Dittus et al. 2017); paradoxically, the open and voluntary nature of these platforms invites a self-selecting participant group, which prompts some to question their representativeness. In an early quantitative study of Wikipedia, Ortega (2009) was among the first to observe that the demographic profile of Wikipedia contributors does not reflect the population average, and also that participation within Wikipedia follows a kind of Pareto principle, where the majority of contributions are produced by a minority of contributors. In other words, not only is the set of participants not repre-

---

2. Their study showed that adding text and photographs to randomly selected articles about small cities led to a 9% increase in hotel visits, worth $190,000 a year.

sentative of the broader population, even among participants themselves there are stark differences in relative contribution volumes.

This is not an unusual finding: in an early, more general, discussion of the promises and limitations of governance on the internet, Nederman et al. (1998) point out that the self-selecting nature of digital communities means that they cannot claim to be representative of the wider population. One cannot expect the outcomes of digital platforms to be inherently fair or representative merely because they are in principle amenable to public participation. Instead, the general expectations should be that, in the words of the authors, 'participants join specialized groups that cater to and reinforce their own interests and even preconceptions'.

Overall, Wikipedia's model of knowledge production has been extraordinarily successful, and its relatively novel volunteer-driven effort has already had an effect far beyond the confines of the site itself. Wikipedia's pages feature prominently in most search engine results, often summarised in a sidebar or infobox (Vincent et al. 2019). As a result, Wikipedia contributes substantially to Google's success: the inclusion of Wikipedia snippets in Google's search results pages arguably has a bigger effect on the perceived quality of the search than many search algorithm improvements (McMahon et al. 2017). Similarly, Wikipedia contributes substantial value to information-gathering platforms like Reddit and the developer community Stack Overflow, where the use of its content was shown to increase visitor engagement and advertising revenue, a relationship that is not necessarily reciprocated (Vincent et al. 2019).

ORGANISING THE INFORMATION

Wikipedia governance as a social process

Being an encyclopaedia – that is, a structured, indexed description of the things that exist in the world – article pages necessarily provide the central organising principle on Wikipedia. Any given topic (e.g. 'Jerusalem') is discussed on a single dedicated page, with more complex topics (e.g. Israeli–Palestinian relations) often spread across multiple interlinked article pages, and perhaps collected into an indexed category of all related articles on the topic. Although multiple perspectives on a topic can coexist within Wikipedia, these are commonly presented within the same article, and as with all contributions, they need to be properly attributed with acceptable sources.

The organisation of information on Wikipedia is inherently a social process. At the most basic level, individuals can contribute by making minor edits to existing articles, by contributing larger pieces of writing, proposing and seeding new articles, or by creating a new article from scratch. All such contributions can be scrutinised by other contributors to ensure they are appropriate and accurate. While in the early days of Wikipedia in the early 2000s this was largely subject to ad hoc judgment calls, today such decisions are made on the basis of detailed content policies that regulate what content is accepted, and how it should be sourced and presented.[3] Contributors may refine or augment any existing contributions, or even revert them (i.e. reverse them) if they deem them to be inappropriate. A publicly visible edit history behind each article provides a historical record of all contributions and reversions for each article. On occasion, disagreements between individual editors can result in significant interpersonal tension (including so-called 'edit wars'), and the ways in which this is addressed procedurally and institutionally is a regular topic for community discourse. At the most basic level, editors can choose to debate an issue on a talk page, that is, a page associated with each article where editors can present their reasoning for particular contributions or reversions. The more severe and intractable disagreements may require outside intervention by a Wikipedian with administrative powers, who can decide what to do, and perhaps even freeze further change to the topic (Sumi and Yasseri 2011).

In the decade since Wikipedia's inception, Wikipedia has started to grow its ambitions to incorporate languages other than English. It now offers 300 translated language editions, which are akin to multiple parallel information ecologies that each present the information in a particular language. The content within a language is often adapted and translated from other language editions; typically English Wikipedia as it is the most comprehensive. But in practice, the Wikipedia language editions are highly heterogeneous in their coverage of content: it has been found that most concepts described in article form only exist in one language, and although English Wikipedia is the largest edition by far, it is not a full superset of any of the smaller language editions (Hecht 2013). Similarly, most images embedded in articles are only referenced from a single language edition, and as a result many language editions

---

3. Nonetheless, inequalities persist. As of 2018, only 17% of biographies in English were about women (Wade and Zainghalam 2018).

have a distinct visual representation of the world that is not shared by others (He et al. 2018).

This difference between language editions is in part also an expression of how they are organised: each has its own contributor community, and the capacity to develop its own content policies. It is likely neither fair nor accurate to think of Wikipedia's language editions as partial translations of a single shared narrative. Instead, each Wikipedia language edition is a cultural sphere that captures a distinct perspective of the world, one that overlaps with other language editions, but also one that can differ in quite significant ways.

Due to this multiply dispersed approach to governance and decision-making, Wikipedia outputs are typically emergent rather than top-down strategy-driven. Although there is a formal non-profit organisation behind the project in the form of the Wikimedia Foundation, it sees itself as the custodian of the technical infrastructure and as a community facilitator, rather than as the sole owner of the project. The Foundation organises regular fundraising drives to collect the financial resources that allow Wikipedia to run as a free and publicly available non-profit information resource. This makes Wikipedia unique among the largest internet platforms: typically, platforms at the scale of Wikipedia rely either on advertising placements or subscription revenue to fund their operations.

Process automation in Google Maps

By comparison, the story of Google Maps is a story about the allure of automation and big data. The platform builds on a data collection effort of immense scale and scope, combined with increasingly sophisticated automated methods of identification and classification. Together they allow Google to produce representations of the world in unprecedented detail. In a striking example, O'Beirne (2017) dissects some of the differences between Apple Maps and Google Maps. Outside of primary urban centres, Apple Maps looks quite empty. In part this is a result of the visual design, but more significantly it is also the result of a difference in content. O'Beirne points out three levels of map detail that allow Google Maps to distinguish itself from the competition: the large-scale collection of building footprints, identification of the specific locations of shops and other businesses, and the aggregation of commercial corridors into 'areas of interest'.

In contrast to most other providers of map data, Google Maps has building outlines for many urban and rural regions. O'Beirne points out that this extends beyond just buildings: Google's maps show the outlines of sheds, garages, park shelters and other structures. Larger structures like churches and office buildings often even include three-dimensional building geometries: towers, roofs, front steps, and so on. In a 2012 press release, the Maps team reveals that these building footprints are algorithmically created from aerial imagery (Parikh 2012). Miller (2014) observes: 'The majority of buildings in the U.S. are now on Google Maps. For landmarks like Seattle's Space Needle, computer vision techniques extract detailed 3D models.' According to statements made by the company, the team had mapped the majority of all buildings in the US within five years, which suggests that the extraction of building geographies from satellite imagery is progressing as rapidly as the collection efforts of Google's Street View vehicles.

Google's 'Ground Truth' project launched in 2008 to extract further geospatial information from satellite, aerial and Street View imagery (Miller 2014; Ibarz 2017). It now provides the specific locations of the shops and other businesses found on Google Maps. Features extracted from Street View include street numbers painted on curbs, the names of businesses and other points of interest, speed limits and other traffic signs, and even turn restrictions that are used for navigation. Compared to a web crawler that discovers information on websites, data collection for Google Maps is about the discovery of new places in the world, locating them not just by address but by physical coordinates.

The overall process is being increasingly automated as it is rolled out to more countries, but it still involves human labour as well as algorithms. Ground Truth is complemented by project Atlas, an in-house human labour force that verifies and refines the information, in part informed by incoming user feedback. Overall, it takes hundreds of human operators to map a country in this manner, resulting in maps of incredible specificity:

> trails have been mapped out and coded as places for walking. All the parking lots have been mapped out. All the little roads, say, to the left of the small dirt patch on the right, have also been coded. Several of the actual buildings have been outlined. Down at the bottom left, a road has been marked as a no-go. At each and every intersection, there are arrows that delineate precisely where cars can and cannot turn.
>
> (Madrigal 2012)

These novel collections of geospatial data then become starting points for a further derivative, the identification of commercial corridors or 'areas of interest': street sections with many restaurants, bars and shops. These are clusters of buildings that host certain kinds of commercial activity. Their spatial geometry is derived not from planning documents or geographic surveys, but from the geometries of street segments and building outlines in Google's geospatial database, cross-referenced with its information about the businesses hosted in each building. The outcomes appear to be highly accurate, and at times even exceed similar surveys produced by humans. O'Beirne provides an example of a 2011 Master's thesis that had identified 27 commercial corridors in San Francisco, which involved a lengthy process reviewing planning documents and interviewing residents. By comparison, by 2017 Google's automated processes had identified all 27 corridors and several more, along with areas of interest for thousands of other cities around the world.

As O'Beirne observes, Google's highly detailed building outlines are by-products of its satellite and aerial imagery, and Google's database of places is partly a by-product of its Street View imagery, which makes Google's areas of interests a by-product of by-products. In other words, 'Google is creating data out of data' (O'Beirne 2017). In these ways, novel geospatial data becomes a competitive advantage: this data is not collected from existing records, it is an original creation. This data has never before existed, and it cannot be replicated by others without requiring the same expensive building blocks.

The merit and the value of these data sets is not merely in their geometries, but also in the semantic mappings they are associated with, all of which become important constituent elements of digital maps. As we have seen, this extends beyond the simple need to display names and labels on digital maps, it is also about the capacity to display rich sets of information that describe locations in ways that are relevant to a person navigating the map, translated into their language. To achieve this, the rich sets of information collected by Google are organised in a complex *knowledge graph, a* semantic information structure that is referenced and interrogated by the processes that construct the final maps.

A GEOSPATIAL PLATFORM ECOLOGY

Now that we have looked at how information is collected and organised by these platforms, we want to spend some time considering the commercial logics behind such operations, with a specific focus on the relationships between Google and other product-driven businesses within the less visible industry of data brokers and other service providers. In this section, we make an attempt to trace the growing geospatial platform ecology that has become the foundation for new digital products of information. We have seen that there is significant infrastructure behind Google Maps. What are the emergent relationships between commercial and non-profit actors, and what do Google and other operators gain from all this effort?

The value chain of digital information

Digital geodata and digital maps have now become basic building blocks within a wide range of products, and a growing ecology of geodata providers is catering to a wide spectrum of information needs, for example by providing the necessary components for the development of urban information overlays. The resulting integrated data products are used by millions, and support a wide spectrum of everyday activities. Digital geodata is used within navigation and transport apps such as Citymapper, Digital Matatus and Transport for Cairo, hospitality platforms like Yelp and Airbnb, but also in social and gaming platforms such as Tinder and Pokémon Go. It is also an essential component in mobility and delivery platforms such as Grab, Gojak and Uber. Although it is typically not made public which of these rely on commercial licensing arrangements with map data providers and which rely solely on freely available geodata resources, it is likely that many of these widely used products have become profitable sources of licensing income for Google and other map data providers.

Beyond these licensed uses of third-party map products, a growing number of organisations are starting to develop their own digital map-making operations. For example, Facebook is producing machine learning technology that traces maps from satellite imagery, Uber is developing increasingly sophisticated cartographic and geospatial infrastructure for their in-house use, and Amazon has started recruiting digital map-making experts.

A significant hidden industry of specialised service providers caters to these digital map-makers, often by providing raw data as discussed earlier in this chapter. In addition, there is a growing need for outsourced human labour within the map-making process, for example when digitising street imagery and satellite data, or when verifying information that was submitted by map users. Lin (2020) offers a fascinating example of the contemporary conditions of a cartographic practice in her portrayal of the work of Indonesian geospatial data technicians. These human map-makers operate as remote workers for a range of clients, and maps are produced from remote sensing data without a capacity to personally experience the mapped places. In her own experience as a digital map worker, Lin also learned about the epistemic challenges of interpreting and representing the world based on such sparse evidence: she calls it 'learning how to see' – learning how to interpret pixels that come in certain patterns and distinguish them from other patterns, in order to then provide them as annotated training data for the machine. In other words, there is a hidden human labour behind digital maps: paid workers in low-wage countries who are tagging and labelling content that ends up in large geospatial databases. The opacity in this value chain means that users never encounter those workers and the workers themselves are rarely told what the end use of their labour is (Anwar and Graham 2020).

From such a vantage point, the various forms of human data contribution we looked at earlier in this chapter could also be considered forms of labour, even if they are unpaid, and not perceived as work – posting reviews, solving Captchas. Similarly, the work of writing Wikipedia, which itself is also part of the larger information ecology, as its outcomes feed into other products, including Google Search. The structured information produced by Wikipedians and by related open knowledge projects is ingested by Google and other platform operators who seek to build semantic databases about the world as part of their geospatial data infrastructure. But in contrast to commercial geodata products that are commonly licensed for a fee, these volunteer-produced data sets – all 'the structured data, categories, and biography articles, images, and so much more' – can typically be used free of charge (Howard 2014).

In other words, Google benefits from the collective labour of Wikipedians at no or little cost. Yet the geodata it derives from such data sources is rarely given away for free. If it is not commercially licensed by third parties, then it is subsidised by prominent advertising placements within map products. Google Maps is a foremost example of this: while it was initially free from advertising, ads are now increasingly visible throughout the product. For example, Google has started trialling the advertising format of 'promoted pins', branded place markers on the map that increase the visual prominence of particular venues, in an effort to 'make location even more central to an advertising experience' (D'Onfro 2016).

These advertising mechanisms in turn inspire and demand further data collection – only this time it is data about people rather than places, in an effort to optimise the highly personalised targeting of ads. Advertising platforms like Google are customers for a vast ecology of data brokers such as Acxiom, Experian, Equifax, Nielsen and Core Logic. These businesses specialise in the collection of data on people, segmenting them in terms of their demographics, consumption behaviours, credit scores and other personal information, and selling the data to other businesses to use in their marketing and advertising (Marr 2017).

One perhaps unexpected outcome of this commercial logic is that Google is increasingly making itself the destination of a search, and a totalising cosmography, rather than the starting point that leads to other websites. In a 2020 review of the structure of Google Search result pages, it was found that a significant and growing part of the first result page is dedicated to what Google calls 'direct answers', summaries of information collected from other sources that are potential answers to the search query (Jeffries and Yin 2020). This capacity to provide immediate answers covers an increasing range of information needs, from dictionary definitions and encyclopaedic summaries derived from Wikipedia and other sources, to more specific information needs relating to currency conversion rates and stock ticker data, weather information, information about diseases and health concerns, and others.

OpenStreetMap as a volunteer-driven map

In addition to these sophisticated commercial efforts, we also want to draw attention to the work of OpenStreetMap, a freely available map of the world that is produced by self-motivated volunteers in a process very similar to that of Wikipedia. OpenStreetMap is noteworthy in multiple respects: just like Wikipedia it is a remarkable achievement of human collaboration at large scale, and with significant outcomes. And just like Wikipedia, the existence of OpenStreetMap points towards the potential for non-commercial models of social knowledge production as an alternative to the commercial efforts discussed in this chapter. Yet in contrast to Wikipedia, OpenStreetMap benefits significantly from the participation of commercial and other institutional users of the data, thus allowing it to bridge two seemingly disparate spheres of knowledge production.

OpenStreetMap was launched in 2004 as a community platform for self-motivated volunteer mappers where in principle anyone can create an account and contribute to the shared global map (Haklay and Weber 2008). Similar to Wikipedia, it follows an open and collective contribution model where arrangements around authorship and ownership are inverted – its geospatial database is freely available to all and communally managed, rather than proprietary and carefully guarded. Contribution to OpenStreetMap requires the use of specialist tools and some specialist knowledge, but significant effort is spent on making this more accessible to newcomers. The platform itself operates as a non-profit with a global governance body, and a growing network of national and regional chapters.

Similar to Wikipedia, this open contribution model has appealed to many. Within the first five years of its existence OpenStreetMap already had tens of thousands of contributors, a number that has since then multiplied many times over. Research has shown that motivations for getting involved in OpenStreetMap are similar to those for Wikipedia. In broad terms these are altruism, access to social experiences, career benefits, self-improvement, ideology and enjoyment of the process (Haklay and Budhathoki 2010; Budhathoki and Haythornthwaite 2013).

Beyond that, it can be argued that OpenStreetMap editors practise a kind of 'pride of place', that they enjoy the opportunity to make maps of their own part of the world. Since its inception, local knowledge has played a central role in the OpenStreetMap value system – the capacity to produce representations of the world based on one's own understanding of it. Consequently, early studies of the OpenStreetMap community have observed that an individual's local geographic knowledge can be the most significant driver to contribute (Budhathoki 2010). This is further augmented by OpenStreetMap's capacity to accommodate regional differences in map representation, for example by reflecting national differences in road classification, or local terminology to describe footpaths and other map features, as observed by Perkins (2014). In this sense, Perkins suggests, OpenStreetMap can be understood as 'a melange of different maps and cultural ways of knowing the world'.

More recently, OpenStreetMap experienced the advent of humanitarian mapping as an innovative extension of this collective practice – we have already discussed an example of this in Chapter 1. Here, aid organisations act in partnership with volunteering networks such as the Humanitarian OpenStreetMap Team to produce maps for humanitarian purposes, typically in response to an emerging humanitarian crisis such as a natural disaster or disease outbreak. Thanks to optimised workflows and large volunteer numbers, new maps of previously unmapped regions can be produced relatively quickly, typically traced from satellite imagery, which means participation is in principle possible from anywhere. This in turn can significantly improve the capacity of aid organisations to provide local support. In other words, these maps can have a significant and life-changing impact on the mapped region. The novel constellation of information needs and volunteering practices in turn introduces a new spectrum of participant motivations – participants are rewarded with a sense of social purpose and the chance to participate in a shared social experience. Their collective contributions can directly help save lives. But humanitarian mapping also introduces a new trade-off: since participation is predominantly remote, the traced maps typically do not benefit from local knowledge, which for example means that road networks can be mapped with some accuracy, however the addition of road names, place names, updated damage assessments, or other more specific map features requires the involvement of local participants.

There are few first-person accounts of what the production of humanitarian maps entails on the ground, and as a result the varied tensions inherent in such work are not always openly acknowledged. David Garcia (2020) offers an early autoethnographic account of the emotional cost of mapping in crisis zones, and the hidden forms of labour involved in volunteer crisis mapping. Garcia describes efforts to map communities in the Pacific that have experienced disaster events caused by climate change, including typhoons, floods and bush fires; the emotional experience of being present in these communities as a map-maker and observer, and the experience of continual suffering and grief. 'Humanitarian work is not a healthy career; it comes with burnout, disappointment, heartbreak' (ibid.). In these crisis mapping efforts, Garcia observes a common insistence on making maps as a first step in the provision of aid, yet finds that the expertise and knowledge practices of local indigenous communities are rarely consulted at this stage. Paradoxically, although the work serves to aid local communities it may simultaneously exclude them from the map-making process. Similarly, when outcomes of these humanitarian efforts are presented to the wider public, the work by and expertise of local mapping communities is not always acknowledged (Vicario et al. 2020).

Overall, it can be said that the OpenStreetMap model of knowledge production is more explicitly organised in terms of terrain and territory, in contrast to the encyclopaedia of Wikipedia which is somewhat detached from it. In OpenStreetMap, discussions and disputes are delegated to local OpenStreetMap chapters if they exist, which means it is in principle possible to address questions around the shared knowledge by means of local expertise, local ownership and local cultural identity. Chapters also organise meetings and communication channels that allow members to discuss and standardise their practices to a degree. At the same time, with the advent of humanitarian mapping this is somewhat complicated – much of the geospatial data is collected from afar, traced from satellite imagery by people without local knowledge, and the complex circumstances of the associated local labour are less readily apparent.

OpenStreetMap has experienced significant growth since its inception almost two decades ago, and has become a key provider of geospatial data. Its open licence permits commercial users to integrate the data into their own maps, as long as the OpenStreetMap community is credited as the original creator of the data. As a result, a rich ecosystem of geospatial organisations relies on and contributes to the data. This includes commercial and non-profit institutions as well as universities who are users of the data, and who can in turn contribute their own resources to the collective production of OpenStreetMap. At its simplest this takes the form of websites and mobile apps such as Maps.me that present a custom rendering of the geospatial data in a streamlined user interface. In addition, its maps are embedded in products such as Craigslist, Snapchat, Tinder and others that display geographic information as part of their interfaces, often via commercial third-party services such as MapBox which offer well-designed renderings of the map. Even Google and other large map producers are known to integrate OpenStreetMap data into their maps. Due to the resulting wide distribution, it is possible that OpenStreetMap-based maps are used as widely as the better-known maps by Apple and Google, even if the users of such maps may not always be aware of this.

In other words, because the geospatial data captured by the Open-StreetMap community is available under an open licence it is finding uses far outside the platform itself, and many of the commercial map providers we have discussed in this chapter are able to integrate Open-StreetMap data in their own maps, thus extending their own map coverage.

This use and integration of the underlying OpenStreetMap geospatial data comes at no cost to the commercial users of the data, but it often requires expertise. As a result, commercial users can become key employers for OpenStreetMap experts who have a deep understanding of the data and the underlying technology, who are often themselves socially embedded within the global OpenStreetMap community, and who then in turn become significant contributors to the platform themselves (Yates and Dodds 2018). In other words, OpenStreetMap manages to integrate or bridge between the somewhat disparate spheres of commercial GIS and self-motivated volunteer mapping. This stands somewhat in contrast to Wikipedia, where commercial contributions are strongly discouraged (M. Graham and Dittus 2018).

TWO COMPLEMENTARY APPROACHES

Digital maps have become an integral part of many digital products and digital experiences across platforms as varied as Waze, Tinder, Google Maps, Pokémon Go, Yelp and many others. There are some real benefits to this seeming omnipresence of digital geospatial information: for many places of the world, today's maps offer a high-fidelity representation of the surrounding terrain, often augmented with highly detailed information overlays that enhance our awareness of our surroundings. But as we have seen, these convenient augmentations are the result of increasingly complex technological and human systems.

Due to significant technology-driven shifts, in recent years we have moved from cartography as a manual craft undertaken by a small number of experts to the coexistence of two parallel practices: on the one hand, a highly automated process of map-making using hand-tuned algorithms and vast heterogeneous data sets, resulting in highly responsive maps of unprecedented detail. On the other, mass-participatory projects to collect human knowledge about the world in the form of discursive social processes.

In comparing those two complementary practices, we are especially interested in comparing them as instances of particular ontological approaches – as ways of describing the world, which in turn then become ways of bringing the world into existence. For example, we can compare their relationships with modes of control. Who gets to participate in the creation of the knowledge, and whose perspectives are represented in the final outcomes? However, these relationships are not simply expressed as a simple binary of a centralised or decentralised approach, rather they are characterised by a set of divergent strategies with respect to a set of different concerns.

Google and Google Maps

If we wanted to identify some essential characteristics of Google Maps we could rightfully call it the most comprehensive and most widely accessible map that has ever existed. And yet we would also need to speak about the fact that seemingly simple processes of looking up information and wayfinding on Google Maps are shaped by a complex set of commercial relations that are not immediately self-evident on the surface. As we have argued, there is no such thing as a neutral map, and Google Maps is no exception. Its vast scale and depth requires significant reliance on automation, and the automated decision-making processes involved in the map-making process are opaque.

Google, as the leading part of the larger Alphabet conglomerate, is one of the world's most valuable listed companies. The company is notoriously secretive about its algorithms, and thus is a strong example of what a strongly centralised and tightly controlled approach to knowledge production looks like. Correspondingly, the geospatial data it produces is commercially licensed, although many uses are free – in particular private and non-commercial, low-volume uses.[4]

Epistemologically, Google's process of geospatial data collection through Street View and other means has been characterised as a kind of 'indexing the world', analogous to the creation of a search index of the internet by crawling links between web pages. The underlying assumption behind these processes is that knowledge about the world can be collected visually and in other automated ways, and that this constitutes an objective capture of the world.

At the same time, Google's representations of the world also recognise complex realities and divergent perspectives. Depending on where you are when you use Google Maps, the borders around the contested Crimean peninsula are marked differently. Google's information architecture allows for multiple perspectives to coexist about any topic

---

4.   Corporations have long played a part in collecting geospatial data. The state-directed Dutch East India Company, for example, heavily invested in map making firms that shaped the geographical knowledge of the time and was essential to the imperialist, capitalist work of the company (see Sutton 2015).

or place of interest. In Google Maps as well as in Google Search, there is rarely a single 'right' answer to any given search. Rather, a well-chosen search term can yield a seemingly infinite number of results. On Google Maps, these results are then often further annotated by customer reviews, a layer of augmentation that allows multiple perspectives about a place to be voiced and heard. This results in knowledge representations of incredible breadth and fidelity.

Yet Google is also confronted with the practical realities of attention scarcity, and in an effort to make the information manageable, its algorithms serve as a way to order and navigate the mass of indexed knowledge. Algorithms use personalisation as a central means of addressing the information flood, algorithmically reordering the complexity into a simple ranked form that attempts to cater to particular information needs and even particular types of people. And it is increasingly attempting to retain this attention within its own platform: as we have seen, a growing amount of space on Google Search result pages is given to direct answers within the search page, rather than pointing outwards to other websites.

This attempt to control reader flows may relate to the central role of advertising as a revenue source for many of the commercial digital map-makers, which becomes a kind of passive income derived from their relative data wealth. The reliance on advertising brings with it: a) commercial incentives to collect data and information about the world so that it can be displayed as content, b) commercial incentives to collect data and information about prospective audiences so that they can be targeted with highly specific ads, c) commercial incentives to prioritise certain target markets over others, based on expected advertising (and other) revenue, but also d) a commercial incentive to retain audiences (or hold them captive, as one might provocatively call it) in an effort to increase advertising views.

Such commercial logics can be considered expressions of *platform capitalism* (Srnicek 2017), an economic calculus that relies on the introduction of intermediaries who benefit from digital transactions, such as the circulation of digital information (Langley and Leyshon 2016). This typically takes the form of so-called multi-sided networks, where the intermediary platform connects networks of producers with networks of consumers, attempting to match the right producer with the right consumer. It is important to recognise that in Google's case, the product being traded is arguably not the information shown on the page, but rather the large numbers of readers of targeted advertising who are being marketed to advertising networks, with Google as the necessary intermediary. This kind of advertising matching necessitates an insatiable appetite for data about the consumer and their preferences (Srnicek 2017). While many services are technically free to users, Google gains a profit from this use by monetising user data.

In other words, Google extracts value from users through every engagement with its products and services: Google and other advertising-supported platforms integrate the free digital knowledge of Wikipedia, OpenStreetMap and other platforms, and use them as starting points for repackaged data derivatives, such as groups of people identified by their interests, which are then traded as commodities with advertisers (Zuboff 2015).

Wikipedia and OpenStreetMap

By contrast, Wikipedia does not rely on advertising – it is run as a non-profit organisation, and relies on fundraising from its readers and other large donors. In its participation model, Wikipedia is decentralised to a significant degree, although it also relies on a significant centralisation of governance. It is highly transparent about its processes, in part as a central strategy to manage the mass-collaborative process, with contributions and governance participation from around the world. The digital knowledge produced by the community is generally available for free, even for commercial use, as long as any reproduction of the work is credited. In other words, Wikipedia is defined by openness in its production model, its model of use, and even its governance.

At the same time, as the project matures Wikipedia is becoming increasingly bureaucratic, and the increasing sophistication of its procedures makes successful participation harder than it was. This is in part due to the fact that Wikipedia's organising epistemology requires a centralisation of knowledge: the wiki structure does not allow there to be multiple articles about the same place or topic. Instead, Wikipedia enforces a consensus view in its representations of the world where all divergent perspectives need to coexist within the same article. This works well as long as all participants cooperate, and as long as more experienced contributors do not abuse their standing in the community in the interest of enforcing particular views. But when disagreements arise, editors might find themselves embroiled in a fight over the 'correct' or 'true' representation, mediated by a complex system of rules and social processes to navigate. By contrast in Google Maps, customer reviews may disagree with each other, but can all share the same space, and disagreements do not need to be resolved. To an extent, the large number of Wikipedia language editions allows for the coexistence of a plurality of cultural standpoints and cultural spheres, and consequently a diversity of representations of the world. However, Wikipedia's language editions are not in an explicit dialogue about their choice of representation, except through the participation of individuals who happen to speak multiple languages and are active in multiple language editions. And, as we will show later in the book, even these many individual editions are the sites of internal conflict and contestation.

This chapter has shown that the DNA of cartography is being restructured. Along with those transformations are new ways in which those cartographies both reflect and shape societies. We have started sketching out some of the emergent tensions, and in the following pages we will explore what kinds of representations of the world are produced as an outcome of these processes. The discussions in this chapter have prepared us to interpret these representations – as we will see, many of the peculiarities and shortcomings of digital representations of the world are a direct result of the complex processes by which digital maps are produced today. We will then return to the question of the production process in Chapter 6, where we consider in more detail who in the world gets to participate in the making of digital maps, and to what extent some of the peculiarities of digital representation are not only expressions of global difference, but also the result of an accumulation of multiple processes of social, economic and political exclusions.

4

A Geography of Digital Geographies

In this chapter we present a first broad empirical inquiry into how place is represented in digital form, drawing from a wide range of examples of digital representations of the world. We first outline some foundational principles of how we can observe and measure such digital geographies. We then investigate the information geographies of Wikipedia, Google Maps and three other public information catalogues that provide digital representations of the world: OpenStreetMap, Geonames and iNaturalist. At this stage we are primarily trying to observe what lies at the surface of such representations: which parts of the world are shown, and how dense with information are these representations?

Our inquiry for this chapter is guided by a broad research question:

- Which parts of the world are represented on contemporary digital platforms?

We operationalise the question with two kinds of measurement:

- How much digital content is there about different global regions, in different languages?
- How has this changed over time?

Each of these aspects reveals a different nuance, gradually deepening our understanding of these representations. While they are informative in their own right, they can also allow us to gauge whether any apparent differences in coverage might be expressions of a systemic inequality in representation. Representation can be a double-edged sword. The increased legibility of populations is historically tied to increased surveillance and subjugation (Mitchell 2002). Yet as the snapshots we outlined in Chapter 1 indicate, there are situations where this coverage is beneficial. In emergency contexts, or around issues of self-determination, inclusion in digital geographies remains a relevant concern.

HOW TO 'MAP' DIGITAL MAPS

There are significant methodological complexities surrounding the measurement of digital maps. Every representation of the world can only ever be a partial account, and every representation of representations even more so. There is no appropriate amount of digital content for a geographic region, and we should be careful about making any normative assumptions about what a 'complete' map looks like. We therefore choose to pursue a kind of strategic essentialism (Eide 2016), to allow for some simplified characterisations of what maps can contain, and how we might observe this, in order to address our concerns relating to digital representation and digital absence. This allows us to offer definitive observations as starting points for constructive discourse. We also acknowledge that this excludes many other important forms of visibility and cultural practice. At the same time, the basic impressions offered by quantitative measurement can become richer if we approach our observations from multiple angles, and if we then bring them into a relationship with additional knowledge, such as the bodies of thought we introduced in Chapter 2, or the procedural practices behind the maps we discussed in Chapter 3.

It is also important to stress that there is no simple correlation between representational invisibility and social, economic or political inequities. Representation alone can never counter forces of inequity. Many people, many groups, and many organisations have important reasons to want to remain unmapped and unrepresented. Our aim is not to suggest that less asymmetrical mappings can somehow undo centuries of accumulated power and privilege, but rather to show the ways that contemporary maps have their own geographies of knowledge.

In this book, we employ two fundamental strategies towards the measurement of content: we measure digital representation in multiple ways (we measure multiple platforms, and different aspects of the same platforms), and we relate our measurements to other observations of the world – at the most basic level, we can relate our observations to the global distribution of the human population, or to the distribution of land surface area. When we then interpret our observations, we must not assume presence and absence happens for the same reasons everywhere, and we must remember that we are looking at a diversity of local communities across a wide range of places, each with their own circumstances. So in this sense, what we present here is best understood as a gradual accumulation of evidence that allows a fuller picture to emerge, rather than a simple answer to a complex question.

A particularly striking example of the measurement challenges we face in this project is the peculiar and somewhat unique status of China within our work. Chinese citizens today represent the world's largest digitally connected population, and Chinese platforms such as WeChat, Alibaba and TikTok are among the world's most widely used platforms. And yet, the Chinese internet is a separate techno-cultural sphere that is almost entirely absent in our explorations. The platforms we selected for this book all have a global focus and an arguably global user base, and yet, as we will see, few of them include detailed representations of China.

THE WORLD ACCORDING TO WIKIPEDIA

As the world's largest web-based encyclopaedia, with the aspiration to collect and make available the 'sum of all human knowledge', Wikipedia is a perfect first candidate for our review of digital representations of the world. How well is Wikipedia fulfilling its ambitious mission? Is it offering comprehensive representations of places across the world? And who, what, and where gets left out?

How to map Wikipedia

When we seek to measure how much information exists on Wikipedia about different places in the world, we immediately run into the problem that information and knowledge are not countable entities. So what should we measure, and how can we measure it? As a first approximation we might count and compare how many articles there are in each of Wikipedia's 300 language editions (that is, how big they are), and we will indeed do so in this book when appropriate. However, because we are particularly interested in the *geography* of digital information, we will count instead the number of articles that have been written *about* particular places in the world, regardless of the languages they are written in.

How can we identify when a Wikipedia article is *about* a particular place? In early iterations of our research we extracted geographic coordinates that had been added to articles by human editors in a range of formats, a process that required significant care and was prone to error (M. Graham and Hogan 2014). Thankfully, in recent years Wikipedians have widely adopted an annotation format for article geotags, a standardised annotation scheme to embed geographic references within

Wikipedia articles. Geotags are not necessarily intended to be read by humans, rather they assist in the automated organisation and presentation of information, for example to display maps within an article. Because of their usefulness they have found widespread adoption on Wikipedia, to a point where we can now rely on them as a good approximation of Wikipedia's overall geography. Figure 4.1 shows geotags being used in an English-language article for the country of Bhutan to denote the geographic centroids of the country and of the capital, Thimphu.

Some measurement challenges remain with this revised approach. A significant limitation of geotags is that they describe points and not regions, and many spatial phenomena and features cannot be easily defined by a simple point (what point would you use to locate Asia, for example?). In practice, spatial phenomena that cover larger regions are commonly described as a single geotag that represents their centroid, rather than a polygon that captures their full extent. Line features such as rivers, in contrast, tend to have coordinates representing their mouth or end. This can mean that a city, river or country is described by a single geographic location. There is also a fairly limited number of extremely large shapes; continents, large rivers, and oceans being the primary ones. While we don't believe that this limitation of geotags will lead to systemic

Figure 4.1   Geotags in the Wikipedia article for Bhutan.

over- or undercounting in our metrics, we do want to bear this limitation in mind.

Just as importantly, we should not assume that Wikipedia has a single dedicated article for all the concepts it describes, nor that all language editions have articles for the same concepts. As we have discussed in the previous chapter, the same concepts may find different articulations in different language editions – which means that topics that are described in a single article in one language might be spread across multiple articles in another, and may simply be a subsection of an article in a third (Hecht 2013). As a result, differences in article quantities between languages may simply be the consequence of different approaches to structuring knowledge. Again, we do not believe that this fundamentally invalidates our measurement approach, however we do want to bear this in mind once we begin to interpret our findings.

Wikipedia's content geography

A map of all geotags on Wikipedia is presented in Figure 4.2, using data from early 2018 aggregated across Wikipedia's 300 language editions, accounting for more than seven million unique geographic locations, including the birth places of notable persons, locations of monuments and other public art, urban as well as natural features, and many other kinds of geographic references. Where the early versions of these maps we produced a decade ago showed many more blank spots – areas with few locations described – we could argue today that Wikipedia is indeed fulfilling its mission to cover the world. That said, we still see clear differences in the degree of global coverage: a high density in much of Europe and North America, and some high-density spots in a few other global regions, but with most of the world appearing to be much less well described. Figure 4.3 shows a more detailed view of Southern Europe and North Africa, where these regional differences in density of description are particularly apparent.

Of course, this is admittedly also a limitation of the visualisation style. Neither people nor notable features are evenly distributed across the Earth's surface (compare the Nile Valley with Egypt's Western Desert, for example) – and so there's no reason we would expect Wikipedia articles to be also.

An alternative attempt to visualise this content geography is shown in Figure 4.4 where we aggregate the data by country. Here, each country

Figure 4.2   The global locations of geotagged articles across all of Wikipedia's language editions. Data: Wikipedia 2018.[1]

1.   Detailed references for our data sources are provided in the Appendix.

Figure 4.3   Wikipedia geotags in Southern Europe, the Middle East and North Africa. Data: Wikipedia 2018.

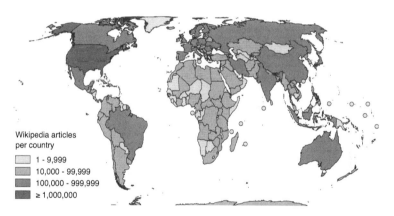

Wikipedia articles
per country

◻ 1 - 9,999
◻ 10,000 - 99,999
◼ 100,000 - 999,999
◼ ≥ 1,000,000

Figure 4.4   Number of Wikipedia articles by country, across all language editions. Data: Wikipedia 2018.

is shaded according to the number of Wikipedia articles that have been written about its places. This visualisation style in some ways evens out spatial concentrations, providing us with a slightly different impression of the global distribution. Overall, the map confirms striking differences in global coverage: North America accounts for by far the largest amount of content, followed by countries in Europe, Asia and parts of South America. Generally, the countries of the Global South are much less well documented than countries in the Global North. African countries in particular receive much less coverage on Wikipedia compared to most other global regions. For example, there are more geotagged Wikipedia articles about Antarctica than about many countries on the highly populated African continent.

In order to put this distribution in context, it is worth displaying the data normalised by both the global distribution of people, and the surface area of each country. Such broad reference points are readily available at global scale, even if only as estimates. Surface area can be derived from satellite imagery and the geometry of national boundaries. An estimate of national surface area is provided by the World Bank in their World Development Indicators data set (a list of all our data sources is provided in the Appendix). We use this as the basis for a normalised map in Figure 4.5. This normalised view does indeed confirm that relative to their surface area, countries in Central and Western Europe and North America tend to have a higher content density on Wikipedia than most other regions of the world, followed by certain countries in South East Asia such as Indonesia, Malaysia, Thailand and Vietnam. By comparison, the representations of South Asia and most of Africa are comparatively thin.

The global population distribution is also available as an estimate at varying spatial resolutions, typically derived from national census data and other disparate sources. For this second comparison we use the Global Human Settlement Layer as a reference (see Appendix), a high-resolution population estimate produced by the European Commission that incorporates evidence from satellite imagery as well as other sources. This allows us to abandon the geometries of national borders as a means of organising our map, and instead to segment space into even-sized hexagonal grid tiles that are more easily comparable. We show the result in Figure 4.6, where we normalise the number of geotagged articles in each grid cell by the estimated local population. Darker shading signifies comparative over-representation of a region relative to its population density, and lighter shading comparative under-representation. A map that perfectly reflects the global population distribution – that is, that showed no variation by underlying population density – would be an even grey. Here, too, we see that Europe and North America are comparatively dense in content relative to their populations, while there is a relative dearth of content in the population hotspots of South Asia (most notably highly densely populated India), China, Central Africa and in other regions of the Global South. This type of visualisation also allows

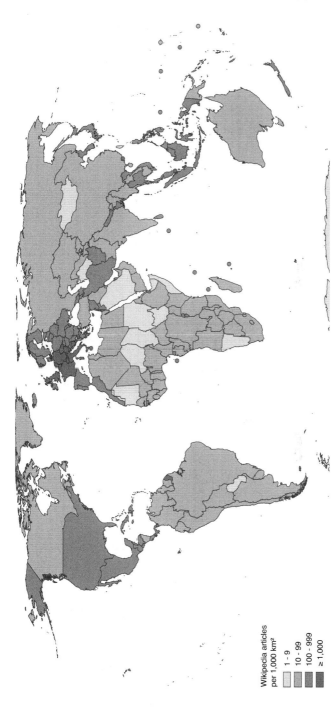

Wikipedia articles
per 1,000 km²

1 - 9
10 - 99
100 - 999
≥ 1,000

Figure 4.5   Number of Wikipedia articles by surface area, across all language editions. Data: Wikipedia 2018.

Wikipedia articles
per capita (million)

0 - 199
200 - 1,999
2,000 - 19,999
≥ 20,000

Figure 4.6 Number of Wikipedia articles per million people, across all language editions. Data: Wikipedia 2018.

us to identify areas of comparatively high content density in essentially uninhabited regions such as the Sahara, the Australian desert, the Antarctic coastline and elsewhere – few people may live there, yet there are still Wikipedia representations of these places.

As a final approach to global measurement and global comparison we simply aggregate these statistics by continent, and compare them. This is shown in the bar chart in Figure 4.7, where we visualise the total surface area, estimated population, and number of geotagged Wikipedia articles for every world region. This level of abstraction allows for quick visual comparison between measures and regions, albeit at the cost of some nuance. This too confirms the overall impression of a significant geographic inequality of representation: significantly more content exists for certain regions of the world than for others. Notably, Europe and North America account for the largest number of geotagged articles, although they are each smaller in population and surface area than other continents, such as Africa and large parts of Asia. In this comparison, the region of Europe and Central Asia (which includes Russia) represents slightly less surface area and a slightly smaller population count than the continent of Africa, yet accounts for approximately four times the digital content. We also see that South Asia is especially poorly represented in Wikipedia.

In summary, through comparison of these relationships – between population, surface area and representation – a more complex picture emerges. Even though these comparisons are simple, we can already see

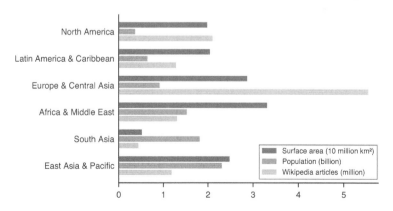

Figure 4.7   Number of Wikipedia articles by global region, compared to population size and surface area. Data: Wikipedia 2018.

multiple dimensions of difference emerging, and multiple expressions of representation inequality. Depending on our vantage point, certain regions appear more or less well-represented. Over the course of the book we will gradually expand this vocabulary of inequality. At this point we simply want to emphasise that such inequalities can be regarded in a number of different ways, each revealing a different set of nuances.

Before resuming our inquiry, we want to briefly take a moment to reflect on the strengths and limitations of these particular choices of measurement. As we cautioned earlier, asking about the distribution of digital information relative to broad reference points like surface area or population is not without issue, and we need to be careful to not assert false equivalences. Just because a country has a greater surface area does not mean we can also expect it to have more features or 'events of note' in it. Rather, its greater size can only ever be used as an indication of a potential or a likelihood. The strength of basic measures like population estimates and surface area are that they are relatively stable measures that are widely used and relatively well-understood and intuitive. This also means that our estimates can be easily reproduced by others, are open to meaningful critique, and are also open to comparisons with other measurement approaches.

We are presented with a further set of choices regarding our approach to spatial segmentation. If we seek to produce measurements that are easily interpretable, aggregating data by country may aid interpretation as it allows us to read the map through the lens of our existing political and historical knowledge of the places described by the data. This might allow us to more easily observe that Germany has a higher article count than Poland, or Iran than Iraq, and we can then begin to start asking questions based on what we already know about those places. (The hex-bins used in Figure 4.6 are of a high enough resolution to allow for this view if we superimpose country borders.)

By contrast, the raw data points shown in Figures 4.2 and 4.3 may be appealing to look at, but are perhaps less useful as a way into detailed interpretation as they do not invite the same kind of relational and proportional reasoning. Yet they too have their place – while raw counts are maybe not that informative in isolation, they often provide a good first starting point to gain an overall impression of the data. At the end of the day, they still show us what the world looks like – at least, according to Wikipedia.

Wikipedia then and now

The spatial inequality in global distribution of Wikipedia content has been known for some time (M. Graham and Hogan 2014; M. Graham, Straumann and Hogan 2015). And to their great credit, both the Wikipedia community and the Wikimedia Foundation have paid close attention to such reports, and have expended much effort in trying to address these inequalities. (We will discuss some of these efforts in more detail in later chapters.) Additionally, Wikipedia contributors are producing new content all the time, and the body of collective knowledge has been growing steadily. Given all of this activity, has the inequality in coverage decreased over time as Wikipedia's overall coverage has increased?

Using our previous aggregates as a starting point, we show in Figure 4.8 how the overall amount of content has grown over time for each region of the world. Overall, we can see clear growth over time. We can also clearly see that representations of places in Europe account for by far the largest number of Wikipedia pages, and that this European content keeps growing at a steady pace. We can also see content growth elsewhere, particularly in recent years where the rate of growth in all major regions has accelerated. For example, African and South Asian

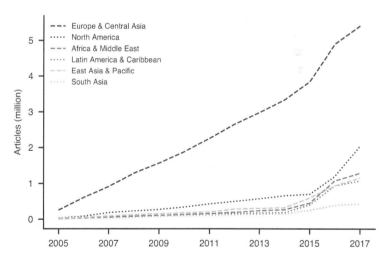

Figure 4.8 Wikipedia content over time, by region, across all language editions. Data: Wikipedia 2018.

content has grown significantly, although they both still lag behind North America. Overall, we can state that coverage is steadily improving, however it is not improving at the same rate everywhere.

If we want to put some of these regional measures in proportion we can compare them relative to Europe, the most content-rich region. By this measure, Europe had 20 times more geotagged articles than all of Africa in 2010. But more recently in 2017, as Wikipedians have vastly increased the amount of content that describes places in Africa, there is now only four times more European than African content. In other words, the coverage gap for Africa has narrowed over time. Of course, it is still worth remembering that the continent has a greater surface area than Europe and a larger population, but is still significantly less well-documented on Wikipedia. Coverage of South Asia and Latin America was initially similarly poor, but has improved since. However, while Latin American coverage is now comparable to that of Africa, South Asian coverage is still trailing behind by a large margin: it has twice the population of Europe, yet only accounts for a tenth of the content compared to Europe.

Languages and multilinguality

Now that we have started to look at geography as a comparative dimension we want to return to the question of language. Similarly to geography, language can provide us with a powerful lens to observe differences in coverage. We have already mentioned in the previous chapter that Wikipedia now has on the order of 300 translated language editions. How comprehensive are they – are the world's languages represented in equal proportion?

In the simplest form we can simply compare how much content is available on Wikipedia in different languages. To put these numbers in proportion we can also factor in the estimated number of speakers of each language, using data from the Ethnologue survey of global languages (Eberhard, Simons and Fennig 2020). We present such a comparison in Figure 4.9, where we compare the number of speakers of the ten most widely spoken languages (including second-language speakers) with the number of Wikipedia articles that have been written in each language. We can see that the amount of Wikipedia content in European languages such as English, French, Spanish, Russian and Portuguese are broadly proportional to the number of speakers, suggesting that these language communities are able to produce a substantial digital representation of

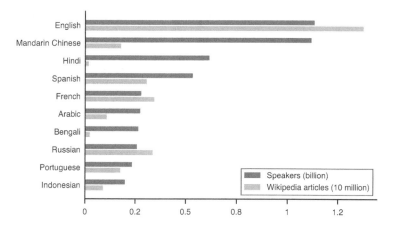

Figure 4.9 Amounts of Wikipedia content for the ten most widely spoken languages. Data: Wikipedia 2018, Ethnologue 2019. Population estimate includes second-language speakers.

the world. But we also see that the other five widely spoken languages are comparatively under-represented: Mandarin Chinese (in Simplified Chinese script), Hindi, Arabic (in the form of Modern Standard Arabic), Bengali and Indonesian are each spoken by hundreds of millions of people, yet each of them accounts for much smaller amounts of content. There are more articles in the French, Spanish or Portuguese Wikipedias than there are in Chinese, Hindi or Standard Arabic – even if some of these account for significantly larger populations. In other words, a review of Wikipedia indicates that the geographic inequality in coverage we observed earlier is accompanied by a linguistic inequality as well: certain languages are much more widely used in digital representations than others. As a consequence, more content exists in some languages than others. While other platforms may have a different linguistic spread, Wikipedia mediates information for a significant amount of internet users around the world.

At the same time, the coexistence of multiple languages on Wikipedia also introduces measurement issues that we need to remain mindful of, as they can lead to measurement inflation. In many regions of the world, the same content can and will exist (by necessity) in multiple languages. This is naturally the case for countries such as Belgium, which has three official languages, and where the local Wikipedia community is active in the Dutch, German and French editions of Wikipedia. In highly multilingual countries like India this can in principle extend to over 20 widely spoken languages. These places will also be written about in other languages, including English. Further complexities arise when languages can be expressed in multiple scripts or is otherwise mixed, such as the transliteration of Arabic into the English alphabet, as well as the use of mixed Arabic and English language in digital communication (Warschauer et al. 2002; Haggan 2007; El-Essawi 2011).

No matter how we approach it, no single measure can easily account for the conceptual complexities around multilingual representation, and we will always need to incorporate multiple forms of measurement to do them justice. Indeed, we will keep returning to the question of multilingual representation in this book.

A GALLERY OF DIGITAL MAPS

Our Wikipedia analyses in the previous sections of this chapter have revealed some of the particular characteristics of the platform's information geography. We now broaden the scope of our analysis to review and compare the information geographies of other platforms. We should note that this is not intended as an exhaustive survey of the internet, instead these are hand-picked examples that will allow us to get a better sense of certain recurring geographic and linguistic patterns.

The geography of Google Maps

As we discussed in the previous chapter, Google Maps is now arguably the most detailed map that has ever existed. Here, we want to trace its information geography in an attempt to interrogate the actual scope of its coverage of the world: how much information is available on Google Maps, and about which places in the world? We want to create a map of Google Maps.

In contrast to Wikipedia, where all information is available for free download, data collection on Google Maps requires significantly more effort. It essentially requires us to probe the search engine with automated search requests, and record the places contained in its responses. In an attempt to capture the global coverage of the platform with some degree of comprehensiveness we repeated this across a large number of locations around the world, and for a large number of different search terms. We will describe the data collection process in more detail in the next chapter, so for now we will simply state that we have crawled hundreds of locations on land worldwide, arranged in a regular grid, and in each location executed queries for dozens of carefully selected search terms, translated into the ten most widely spoken languages worldwide. In total, our global scan of Google Maps required 1.4 million search queries, and returned tens of millions of search results, identifying around three million unique 'places'.

Figure 4.10 shows the global distribution of all the places we discovered on Google Maps using these methods, including restaurants, bars, parks and other urban amenities. While the total size of Google's geospatial database is unknown to us (although it is obviously vast), the map provides a basic estimate of the relative global *distribution* of its coverage. Due to the way this data was collected it only provides us with a relatively coarse spatial distribution, especially when compared to the high-resolution coverage map of Wikipedia in Figure 4.2. And yet, we can see a shared resemblance: there is excellent coverage of the Global North, in particular North America and Central and Western Europe. Many parts of the Global South are strikingly well-covered as well, in particular India, China, and large parts of South America, compared to Wikipedia's coverage. So, overall the distribution suggests that Google Maps is covering much of the world. But in comparison with other global regions, many African countries are not so well represented. A significant part of the African continent has much lower content density than, for example, many European or North American countries.

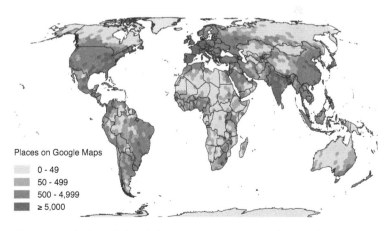

Places on Google Maps

- 0 - 49
- 50 - 499
- 500 - 4,999
- ≥ 5,000

Figure 4.10   Estimated Google Maps coverage, aggregated across the ten most widely spoken languages. Data: Google Maps 2019.

While these distributions are fascinating in their own right, they do not as yet allow us to assess the extent to which they might reveal systematic inequalities of representation. For such an assessment we should refer instead to Figure 4.11, which shows the population-normalised version of this distribution. We can see that normalisation of the data (i.e. controlling for population density) has two effects. First, we can see an overall reduction in coverage differences: there are fewer regions that are either extremely well-covered, or extremely poorly covered. This suggests that Google Maps' global coverage does indeed reflect the global population distribution, where more densely populated places tend to (naturally) show more elements on the map.

But we can also see a secondary effect which speaks to our question of inequality. The maps for North America, parts of Western Europe, parts of South America and Australia seem fairly dense. By comparison, Central America, Eastern Europe, large parts of Asia and most of Africa only have a fraction of this content, relative to their population density. In particular, the 'hotspots' of India and China we saw in Figure 4.10 have blended in with their less well-represented neighbours: relative to their high population density, Google's maps are not always as detailed here as they are for Europe and other parts of the Global North. And again, large parts of Africa are among the least well-covered places in the world, relative to their population density.

These differences may appear to be relatively minor, however there are much more striking coverage inequalities that become apparent once

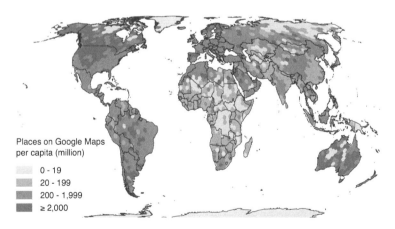

Places on Google Maps
per capita (million)

- 0 - 19
- 20 - 199
- 200 - 1,999
- ≥ 2,000

Figure 4.11   Estimated Google Maps coverage, normalised by population.
Data: Google Maps 2019, GHSL 2019.

we start to examine Google Maps' coverage across languages. Not all of its mapped content is available in all languages. Rather, depending on the language used to search, Google Maps returns different subsets of its complete geospatial database. Of the three million unique places we discovered through our automated querying, around half were discovered with English-language searches, following a global distribution that closely resembles the one in Figure 4.10. By comparison, only around a quarter of these places were included in the results for French, Spanish, Russian and Portuguese searches, and only a tenth in the search results for Indonesian, Arabic and Mandarin Chinese. In other words, language populations that arguably represent a significant part of the global majority are comparatively underserved – they are only shown a fraction of the content, and consequently only have access to a fraction of all representations of the world. However, maybe the most striking inequality is experienced by speakers of Hindi, who were shown less than 5 per cent of the global map, and Bengali, who only have access to less than 1 per cent of the global map. This is particularly surprising because Hindi is the world's third most widely spoken language, and Bengali the seventh, each spoken by hundreds of millions of people. This vast discrepancy is illustrated in Figure 4.12, where we compare the total number of language speakers to the number of locations we discovered on Google Maps for each of the ten languages.

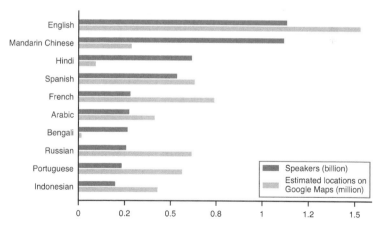

Figure 4.12 Google Maps content volumes for the ten most widely spoken languages. Data: Google Maps 2019, Ethnologue 2019. Population estimate includes second-language speakers.

These vast coverage inequalities across languages are also reflected in the spatial dimension, and they are experienced by some more than others. Figure 4.13 shows the spatial distribution of all search results for four languages: Arabic, English, Hindi and Spanish. The distribution of English-, Arabic- and Spanish-language content broadly appears to resemble the overall distribution in Figure 4.10, with the Arabic map having comparatively better coverage of the Middle East and North Africa, and the Spanish map better coverage of South America. However, the Hindi-language map shows a striking spatial clustering: Hindi content is largely constrained to the Indian subcontinent, as is Bengali (which is not shown here). In other words, the utility of Google Maps for speakers of Hindi or Bengali is highly dependent on location, and speakers of these languages would not be able to navigate most of the world in their native language. (As we will see in Chapter 5, the practical reality of these language geographies on Google Maps can be even more challenging.) In other words, the vast majority of Google Maps content is only accessible to English speakers; and among the most widely spoken languages, coverage is notably poor for speakers of Hindi and Bengali.

We will investigate the information geography of Google Maps in more detail in Chapter 5, where we will also explore its coverage at local scale. For now, we simply observe that the global spatial coverage of Google Maps is maybe less highly concentrated on certain regions of the Global North when compared to Wikipedia, although we can still identify many of the same concentrations and absences. This pattern is further amplified by a coverage inequality across languages, where speakers of the major languages of the Global North have access to a larger amount of content than speakers of other global languages.

OpenStreetMap and other digital maps

To complement these first broad impressions, we will briefly look at the information geographies of three additional platforms that focus on the collection and dissemination of digital geodata: OpenStreetMap, Geonames and iNaturalist. Following our approach of the previous maps we present their content distributions as population-normalised and hex-binned maps, rather than merely showing the raw data. This means relative over-representation is visible as darker shading, and relative under-representation as lighter shading. A consequence of the population normalisation is that certain aspects are exaggerated in these maps

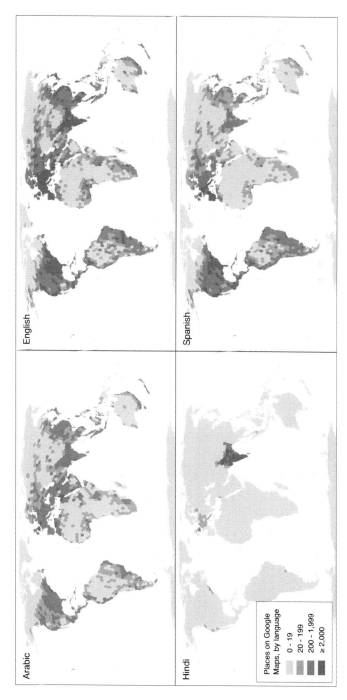

Figure 4.13 Estimated Google Maps coverage for four widely spoken languages: Arabic, English, Hindi and Spanish. Data: Google Maps 2019.

– in particular, small amounts of content in population-sparse regions appear as highly content-dense. We can see this most clearly in the Sahara region.

Figure 4.14 shows the global content distribution of OpenStreetMap as of early 2020. We discussed the platform in the previous chapter – it is a volunteer-produced map following a process similar to Wikipedia, largely relying on local volunteers as well as remote participants tracing satellite imagery. Due to its open licence, OpenStreetMap data is used in the production of maps by Google, Apple and others. Looking at its information geography we can see a similar distribution to many of the earlier examples; indeed, the map almost perfectly matches the population-normalised distribution of Wikipedia in Figure 4.6. In particular, India and China are strongly under-represented relative to their high population density, while Europe and North America are highly prominent. Africa sits somewhere in between these – many African countries have an order of magnitude less content than many places in Europe, relative to the population.

In Figure 4.15 we visualise the content distribution of Geonames as of early 2020. Geonames is an instance of a gazetteer, a curated information directory about places in the world. Available as a free download and with an open licence, it is used widely as a reference data set, for example during the creation of software that needs to identify geographic locations for named places such as countries or cities. The map shows that the global content distribution of Geonames is very similar to that of OpenStreetMap, including the relative absence of India and China due

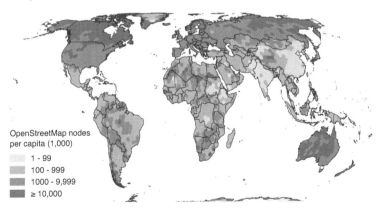

Figure 4.14   Number of nodes in OpenStreetMap per thousand people. Data: OpenStreetMap 2020, GHSL 2019.

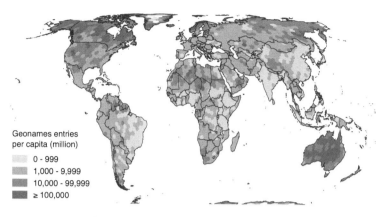

Figure 4.15 Number of entries in the GeoNames database per million people. Data: GeoNames 2020, GHSL 2019.

to the proportional scaling, and the relative absence of Central and West Africa.

Figure 4.16 shows the content distribution of iNaturalist in early 2020. iNaturalist is a citizen science platform that solicits plant and animal observations from volunteers around the world, in an effort to map the global flora and fauna and make the information freely available. In contrast to the earlier maps, here the spatial distribution is highly unequal: North America and Europe are highly dense with observational reports, as is South Africa. Yet most other regions of the world are comparatively under-represented, especially across Africa and Asia. Among all the

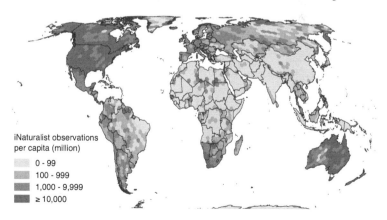

Figure 4.16 Number of observations in iNaturalist per million people. Data: iNaturalist 2020, GHSL 2019.

digital representations of the world discussed in this chapter, this is by far the most highly unequal. It is not immediately evident why its coverage differs so much from that of the other platforms; possible drivers include that this data is collected by a comparatively small and special-interest community, that the platform has a specific focus on English-language content, and that the citizen science practice of volunteer observations of nature may not be of interest to global audiences. (It may be worth mentioning that we could have normalised the iNaturalist coverage data by surface area, given it describes natural phenomena. But in this particular case we are primarily interested in the map as a social artefact produced by human activity, and we want to keep it comparable to the previous maps, so we chose to normalise by population.)

A GLOBAL MAP?

In this chapter we have measured and compared the digital representations produced for places around the world across a range of platforms to better understand their spatial distribution. Are certain regions more well-represented than others? We find that platforms do vary in their spatial coverage, however also that they are often strikingly consistent in which places they over- or under-emphasise.

Overall, we find that *digital information now covers the globe* – the digital representations of the world on Google Maps, Wikipedia, OpenStreetMap and Geonames capture every continent and most global regions in some degree of detail. Among all platforms we have reviewed, Google Maps has maybe the most even global coverage – which may be a direct consequence of the significant resources and expertise behind their maps, as discussed in Chapter 3. But also Wikipedia, whose coverage a decade ago showed many more dark spots, is arguably today fulfilling its mission to capture the world's knowledge – at least when seen from this high-level vantage point of global geographic coverage.

And yet, we also find *stark inequalities of representation*, and all of these geospatial databases still place a relative emphasis on certain regions at the expense of others. The patterns of unequal coverage are surprisingly similar across platforms – we generally see a high density of content in Central and Western Europe and in North America, and some high-density spots in a few other global regions, but relative under-representation in most of the rest of the world, particularly countries of the Global South, and especially in South Asia and Africa. Even Google has significant geographic blind spots, and its coverage of African countries is still highly sparse. The same is true for Wikipedia – the region of Europe and Central Asia (with Russia) has slightly less surface area and a slightly smaller population than Africa, yet approximately four times the digital content. These inequalities of coverage hold even if we account for the world's unequal population distribution, and in some regions they become more severe – compared to their population sizes, the highly densely populated regions of South Asia and China tend to be under-represented on Wikipedia, Google Maps and all other platforms we surveyed.

The unequal spatial coverage is further amplified by a linguistic inequality, that is, a highly unequal coverage across languages. On the platforms we surveyed, there is much more digital content available in European languages than in other widely spoken languages such as Hindi and Bengali. Overall, even on highly multilingual platforms like Wikipedia and Google Maps there is a limited set of content-rich languages. Native speakers of under-represented languages may be confronted with a choice to switch to one of the more widely supported languages if they want to engage with digital representations of the world.

However, we can also see that digital coverage is improving over time, and that this often benefits under-represented regions. On Wikipedia, we have seen clear improvements in coverage of under-represented regions, particularly in recent years, and as a result the existing coverage gaps are slowly narrowing. Where ten years ago there was 20 times more European content on Wikipedia than content about Africa, there is now only four times the content. Digital inequalities are slowly narrowing.

Now that we understand these basic relationships, we want to gradually refine our understanding of these differences in representation over the following chapters. In Chapter 6 we will attempt to identify the many systemic factors that conspire to produce such outcomes, including the many barriers to entry and other forms of exclusion that prevent broad-based participation. In Chapter 7 we will give specific examples of the epistemic injustice that can arise from this, asking questions about who gets to participate in the creation of knowledge, what kind of knowledge is produced as a result, and what claims about the world are made. Finally, in Chapter 8 we will summarise the broader social justice concerns we encounter in digital representation, and offer strategies to counteract them and develop more just representations.

But first, we want to concretise some of the ways in which representation inequalities can affect our everyday interactions with digital maps in practice. Our findings in this chapter suggest that not everyone receives the same coverage, and we want to develop a better understanding of what this actually looks like in practice. When we use Google Maps to navigate our own city, do we all see the same map?

5

Digital Augmentations of the City

The previous chapter described the global coverage of digital maps, across a range of examples from Wikipedia and other platforms. This has provided us with a first sense of the stark global differences within digital information spaces: unequal geographic coverage, an apparent over-representation of certain languages, and under-representation of others. Prompted by these striking spatial and linguistic divides in global digital representation, we now seek to better understand whether these are simple differences or real inequalities. To what extent do these differences in representation mean that different populations receive different perspectives of the same places? Can we find instances where information absences become forms of exclusion?

In an effort to better understand the potential effects of digital representations on everyday experiences, in this chapter our inquiry is linked to concrete uses of the digital map at the urban scale. Using Google Maps as a case study, we compare its representations of a selection of cities around the world, asking to what extent maps presented in different languages also differ in their representations of the world. While we cannot expect that all of the world is represented in all languages, we can ask whether representations of a particular place exist in its local languages.

Our inquiry in this chapter is guided by a central research question:

- Do the same maps in different languages differ in their representations of the world?

We operationalise the question with two complementary forms of measurement:

- How much map content is available in different languages?
- To what extent are search results available in *local* languages?

In contrast to Wikipedia where we can access the full data set for analysis, the geospatial database behind Google Maps is a proprietary data set that is only ever revealed to us in parts, for example in the form of a local map or search result. As a consequence, to interrogate how Google Maps represents the world requires us to change our data collection approach. As already mentioned in the previous chapter, for this study we executed search queries for a large number of locations around the world, translated into dozens of languages. We then compare the search results, and discuss the representations of the world they provide. In other words, we probe and critique Google Maps by comparing it to itself, using language as a proxy to observe and compare the experiences of different population groups.

To support this comparative approach, we study the maps of eleven global cities – that is, multilingual urban regions where multiple language communities coexist in various forms. Seven of these cities are officially multilingual,[1] where each has multiple officially recognised local languages. These are Brussels in Belgium, Dar es Salaam in Tanzania, Montréal in Canada, Nairobi in Kenya, the Hong Kong urban region, Kolkata in India and Tel Aviv in Israel.[2] To complement this selection, we have selected four cities that are officially monolingual but that host significant populations speaking a range of different languages. These are New York City, Berlin, London and São Paulo. Those urban scans are then complemented with a large-scale global scan of Google Maps, at much coarser spatial resolution, and for a subset of the most widely spoken global languages, in order to compare content distributions at global as well as regional scale.

HOW TO MAP GOOGLE MAPS

Search queries as digital probes

Google Maps is a challenging system to study and interpret. We can only really observe it by asking it questions (i.e. submitting search queries),

---

1.   We rely here on a data set of national languages by the Unicode consortium, which distinguishes between official languages (by law) at the national level, official languages (by law) at the regional level, and de facto official languages. In this chapter, we consider all these to be instances of 'official' languages (see Appendix).

2.   Hebrew is the official national language of Israel, but Arabic is recognised as a language of special status, and has historically had the status of an official language.

and noting the answers that come back. The basic principle can be illustrated with a simple example.

Figure 5.1 shows a screenshot of an Arabic-language search for restaurants in Kafr Qasim, a city in Israel near the border with the West Bank. Like every Google Maps search, the underlying search query is constituted from two basic parts: a geographic location (i.e. from which the query was made), and an information need that is expressed as a set of search terms in a particular language. The screenshot also shows a set of search results, visualised both as pins on the map and as a results listing on the side. Each individual search result represents a particular place, such as a restaurant or shop, and tends to be presented in a language which may or may not be different from the search language. In this case – an Arabic language search for a restaurant, or 'مطعم' – we can see results presented in Arabic, Hebrew and English, all within the same search result listing. In total around two dozen venues have been suggested, all within walking distance of where the query was launched.

For our global data collection, we systematically executed millions of such Google Maps searches across multiple languages, search terms and locations, and collected and compared the search results that came back. This allows us to trace the geospatial and geolinguistic contours of Google Maps through this large number of automated search queries.

Figure 5.1   Results of an Arabic-language restaurant search in Kafr Qasim, near the West Bank.

In order to avoid the effects of algorithmic personalisation – that is, the fact that Google will learn users' preferences and interests over time and personalise the results to them – we prepared a clean session without any prior search history for each data collection pass. This is in part a pragmatic attempt to maintain a simple study design that can easily be replicated by others.

Search languages and search terms

For the selection of global cities we identified local languages that are either recognised as an official language at national or regional level, or are spoken by a significant subset of the population. (The full set of languages per city is shown in Figure 5.2.) Rather than attempting comprehensiveness we only selected a subset of languages, in part informed by our own understanding of these places. For example, for Berlin we selected German, English and Russian as languages of interest. Although French, Italian and other European languages are more widely spoken across Germany, we specifically wondered to what extent Russian coverage on the map might reflect the post-war split of the city into West and East Berlin.

Further, for an analysis of the global contours of Google Maps we selected the ten most widely spoken global languages, according to the Ethnologue corpus of languages spoken around the world. In total, we selected 23 languages for inclusion in our study: Afrikaans, Arabic, Bengali, Cantonese (in Traditional Chinese script), Catalan, Dutch, English, French, Galician, German, Guaraní, Hebrew, Hindi, Indonesian, Italian, Malay, Mandarin (in Simplified Chinese script), Portuguese, Russian, Spanish, Swahili, Xhosa and Zulu.

We then identified 44 English search terms that would allow us to discover content in Google's geospatial database. Informed by the taxonomies of similar geospatial databases we curated a list of urban affordances that are commonly encountered in cities around the world, including restaurants, schools, parks and other potential destinations. We included a range of urban features that have high spatial density such as shops and schools, while also including public amenities such as parks and universities that may be less frequent within a city, but that are commonly found in cities. (The full list of terms is provided in the Appendix.)

We translated these search terms into each of the target languages with the help of both professional and volunteer translators, recruiting one or

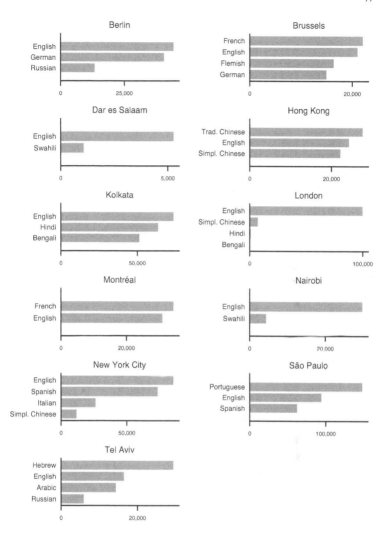

Figure 5.2 Map coverage by location and search language. Showing the number of unique places discovered through different searches. Data: Google Maps 2019.

more volunteer translators and one professional translator per language. Translators were given a detailed briefing, and asked to choose terms that would be used for a map search by a native speaker of the respective language. In the briefing we acknowledged that different people might use different terms for the same information needs, and left it up to the translator to choose their preferred tone of voice. In cases where translators offered multiple alternative translations for a term we included all variations in our final search corpus. This combined and comprehensive approach provided us with some confidence in the formal correctness of the translated corpus, while also allowing for a variety in search strategies. In total, we received around 1,300 translations, adding up to a search corpus of around 1,350 search terms, including the original English terms.

Data collection

In order to cover larger regions of interest in our sample, searches were organised in spatial grids. Within each urban region we constructed an even-spaced grid of locations from which to search for local amenities, covering both the urban centre as well as part of the suburban ring. The search grids were constructed at relatively fine spatial resolution, limiting each grid to hundreds or at most low thousands of search locations. In most cities, our individual search locations are at most hundreds of meters apart. We chose a coarser grid spacing of 1.2 km for three cities that spanned a geographically larger region: Montréal, Nairobi and São Paulo. We executed Google Maps searches at more than 9,000 sample locations across the eleven cities, sending search requests for terms in each city's languages of interest. This resulted in two million search queries executed across the eleven urban regions.

For a separate global scan we constructed a regular worldwide grid at an average grid spacing of approximately 160 km, accounting for 2,600 sample points over land. Data collection for the global scan required 1.5 million searches to cover the ten most widely spoken languages. The data collection took place over a period of approximately two months.

Search result listings provided us with information about the locations, or 'places', known to Google Maps. The metadata for each individual search result contains a full description of the places listed. This includes a name for the location or venue, a geographic location as both geographic coordinates as well as a street address, and an identifier code that uniquely identifies the particular 'place' within Google's geospatial database. It may also include additional metadata such as a homepage URL, and a set of category labels. Finally, each search result includes a designation of the language in which the search result is described, which allows us to compare whether the result language matches the language of the search request.

THE CITY ACCORDING TO GOOGLE

We can estimate the overall spatial distribution of Google's geospatial database by aggregating the search results from our millions of queries. This gives us an indication of which parts of the world are known to Google Maps, and allows us to compare the extent to which this coverage differs between languages. We express this in two complementary measures: as search result volume, which is the aggregate volume of search result listings for our searches in a given region of interest, and as content density, which is the unique number of 'places' identified by Google Maps across these search results, as identified by their unique identifier code.

Gaps and omissions

During early test crawls it emerged that several regional languages we wanted to include in our study are not represented on Google Maps, and as a result it was not possible to offer a comparative survey of the cities in which these languages are spoken. We made attempts to assess the Google Maps coverage in the South African languages Xhosa and Zulu, and the Paraguayan language Guaraní, but in all three cases found that the languages were not represented on the map. Instead, the cities where these languages are spoken are represented in English and Afrikaans, Spanish or other majority languages of the respective regions. This gives the impression that Google Maps is not available to speakers of Xhosa, Zulu and Guaraní, and potentially to speakers of many other regional languages spoken by millions. Instead, speakers of such unsupported languages have to switch to other languages in order to navigate the map. We consider this a significant omission: according to Ethnologue, Xhosa is spoken by an estimated 8 million people (19 million including second-language speakers), Zulu by an estimated 12 million (28 million including second-language speakers) and Guaraní by an estimated 6 million.

Local content density

A first basic outcome of our data collection is a general impression of the urban information density on Google Maps. How much map content is available in different languages? As outlined above, for every city we executed map searches for dozens of search terms across a small number of languages spoken in the city. We then collated all unique places identified in the search results returned from these queries, which gives us a basic estimate of the map coverage of the city in the respective languages. Figure 5.2 shows the map coverage across locations and languages, measured as the number of unique places discovered through these searches.

In officially multilingual cities there is a relatively balanced coverage between local languages. In Montréal we discovered around 34,000 unique places using French searches and 31,000 unique places using English. Similarly, in Hong Kong coverage is relatively even between English (around 24,000 unique places), Mandarin Chinese in Simplified Chinese script (22,000 places), and Cantonese in Traditional Chinese script (27,000 places). In Brussels, coverage is relatively even between local languages French (22,000), Flemish (16,000) and German (15,000), and even English (21,000), which is not an official local language. These results represent the expected outcome for many of the surveyed locations: in these multilingual cities, we see relatively balanced content density across the major languages spoken.

Going a step further, we can see the spatial distributions of the places discovered per language in Figure 5.3, which examines the data density

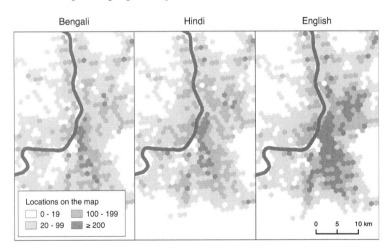

Figure 5.3   Content density in Kolkata for Bengali, Hindi and English. Measured as the number of unique destinations discovered through map searches in these languages. Data: Google Maps 2019. River features: OpenStreetMap 2020.

of the city of Kolkata in north-east India. We surveyed three languages that are used locally in Kolkata: Bengali is a local official language (51,000 unique places discovered), Hindi a national official language (63,000 places), and so is English (73,000 places). All three languages are relatively well-represented in terms of map coverage, although English has the most content – a European language that was originally introduced to the region through British colonialism, but which is now in everyday use across the region. We can see that content in all three languages follows a similar spatial distribution, and the higher data density of the English map is readily apparent. This kind of spatial pattern is typical for the cities we surveyed, in that the general spatial distribution of map data is often comparable between languages, however data volumes might differ – and as we will see soon, they can differ quite significantly.

To an extent, we see similar outcomes in cities with significant unofficial minority languages, although this varies by place and by language. In New York City, searches in English revealed the highest map density (85,000 places), however we also discovered a large amount of Spanish-language content (73,000). On the other hand, we discovered very little content in Mandarin Chinese (12,000 places). This is broadly reflective of the local demographic distribution, where Hispanic Americans or Latinos represent as much as a third of the local population, while Asian Americans represent a much smaller subset. We observe a similar distribution in São Paulo, where most of the discovered content is in Portuguese (148,000 places), while there is also a significant volume of English- and Spanish-language content available (94,000 and 62,000 places, respectively). Yet in comparison to the majority language Portuguese, the map is much less dense in these local minority languages.

In Tel Aviv, the most content-rich language is Hebrew (30,000 places), but there is also much content in Arabic (14,000) and English (16,000), while we only found little content in Russian (6,000). In other words, the map of Tel Aviv is significantly less content-rich when navigated in Arabic than in Hebrew. To an extent this reflects the local demographic distribution, where Jews represent the majority population of Tel Aviv, Arabs a significant minority, and other population groups only a small percentage. Yet this also means that speakers of Arabic are only shown a subset of the map that is available to Hebrew speakers.

By contrast, the map for London is predominantly English (100,000 places), while only a small fraction of the map is available in Asian languages (Bengali: 120 places, Hindi: 700, Mandarin: 7,100). This may be unexpected if we consider that as much as a fifth of the local population is of Asian descent, about half of that with South Asian origin. However, it possibly simply reflects the fact that this is a functionally monolingual city, where most residents are fluent, or at least proficient, in English, and second- and third-generation migrants predominantly speak English in everyday use.

Maybe more surprisingly, this prevalence of English-language content even extends to Berlin, where English is the most content-rich language on the map (44,000 places), with German content density slightly lower (40,000 places) – even though English does not have the status of an official language, neither at regional nor at national level. By comparison, much less Russian content is present in Berlin (13,000 places), possibly reflecting the fact that this language is not in everyday use, even if a significant subset of the population is still able to speak it.

However, there are also significant content gaps in certain languages. This is particularly evident with Swahili. It is an officially supported interface language in Google Maps, yet very little Swahili content is present even in places where it is used as an official language. In Dar es Salaam in Tanzania the map reveals a high volume of English content (5,300 places) compared to Swahili content (1,100 places), even though Swahili is more widely spoken by the population. In Nairobi in Kenya the difference is similarly striking, with a very high volume of English content (30,000 places), and Swahili content only representing a fraction of that (4,300). As a result, the Swahili-language maps of these cities are comparatively empty, and possibly unusable for certain information needs. For example, a search for the English term 'restaurant' shows results in both cities, while the Swahili equivalents 'mkahawa' or 'mgahawa' show none. Confusingly, Swahili-language terms *do* appear in the English-language search results, where they are correctly labelled in Swahili as 'mkahawa' (restaurants). In other words, there is a discrepancy between the search user interface (which uses Swahili terms), and the geospatial database which appears to lack Swahili content. As a consequence, Swahili speakers are confronted with a peculiar paradox: while they can use the application in their own language, they will need to use English search terms to discover key parts of the city.

In summary, this confirms our observations of the previous chapter at the local level: content in a lot of languages is relatively absent from urban augmentations. Even when navigation interfaces support a particular language, content may still be missing in those languages.

Mixed-language search results

Figure 5.1 illustrated how, in some cases, search results can contain a mixture of languages. In the case shown – the Israeli city of Kafr Qasim, close to the West Bank – it was a mixture of Arabic, Hebrew and English. How often does this happen? That is, how often do searches in one language include results in another? Given that individual search results on Google Maps are annotated with an automated assessment of the language they are written in, we can use this as a basis for our analysis. Instead of estimating content density, or the unique number of places that are known to Google, for the analysis of mixed-language results, we instead consider how this content is presented in the results. To this end we aggregate the number of search results shown on the first results page (i.e. the first 20 results) across all searches in a given language, and determine whether the results are provided in the search language or in a different one.

Figure 5.4 offers an aggregate view of how often search results include content in a language other than the search language. It shows the aggregated volume of search results per location and language, and indicates the subset of these search results which are presented in the same or a different language.

We can see that in officially monolingual cities like Berlin, São Paulo and New York City, the local official language is typically also the most prevalent language in terms of search result listings, even when searching in other languages. In Berlin, few results for Russian-language searches are actually presented in Russian – instead, 70 per cent of these results are in German, and 25 per cent in English. Similarly, in São Paulo, 70 per cent of English- and Spanish-language search results are actually presented in Portuguese. And despite our earlier figures about New York which suggested the presence of a large volume of Spanish-language content, Google's presentation of the city actually appears to be extremely monolingual: more than 90 per cent of the results for Spanish-language searches are presented in English. Overall, this suggests that either Google Maps seeks to offer content in a language independent manner, supported by an effort to translate search queries; or alternatively, that it even makes an effort to substitute content in other languages instead of showing empty result pages when content is not available in a given language.

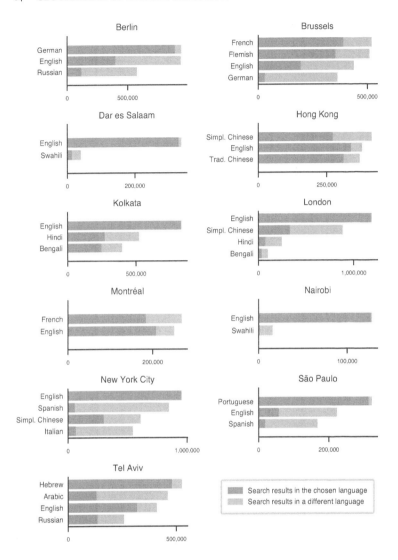

Figure 5.4   Aggregated volume of search results by place and language. Indicating the share of foreign-language content. Data: Google Maps 2019.

In multilingual cities, results in the respective official languages all have some degree of mixed-language content, typically also involving other local official languages. For example, in Montréal about a third of French search results are presented in English, while 15 per cent of English search results are shown in French.

However, depending on the city, the relative proportion of available content is not always balanced between all local languages, and neither is the impact on search result listings. For example, in highly multilingual Brussels, foreign-language results for searches in Flemish or German are almost twice as likely to be presented in English than French. For Flemish-language searches, 20 per cent of all results are in English compared to 10 per cent in French. For German searches, 50 per cent of results are in English and 20 per cent in French. Overall, these numbers suggest that in Brussels, English-language content is often given preference when filling in content gaps in other languages, despite not being an official language of this city. (Yet as we will see later, in principle there is more French-language content available.)

In some cities, these measures reveal a striking coverage and representation gap between languages. In Tel Aviv we find little Arabic-language representation in search results. Of all Arabic-language searches, almost 60 per cent of search results were in Hebrew, 12 per cent in English. Even Swahili coverage is much worse than our initial numbers suggested. In Dar es Salaam, 70 per cent of Swahili-language search results are actually presented in English, and in Nairobi this number grows to a striking 90 per cent. In Kolkata, we find Bengali and Hindi are less well-represented in search results than it initially appeared, while English is highly prevalent: almost 40 per cent of results for Bengali-language searches and 50 per cent of results for Hindi-language searches are actually in English.

Overall, the picture drawn by these distributions appears to complement the language distribution inequalities we saw earlier: foreign language results are often an attempt to fill content gaps in cases where less content is available. Consequently, such substitutions are often in the language in which most local content is available, which varies by city. In places like London, New York or Berlin it is the primary official language – English or German, respectively. In officially multilingual cities like Montréal or Brussels it can be either of the official languages. However, in Dar es Salaam, Nairobi and Kolkata, English content is by far the most prevalent in search results – even when searching in other languages that are much more widely spoken by the local population.

Local language geography

The evidence discussed so far points to huge imbalances in how content is distributed in different languages. We have also shown that search results can include a significant amount of content in foreign languages. As a result, it is worth estimating our earlier content density measures in a stricter manner. In order to do this, we now estimate local content density while excluding any foreign-language content. This allows us to update the results from the previous analysis with more specificity – rather than estimating the total amount of content that is available to searchers in a given language, we now only estimate the subset of content that is actually written in the particular language.

To illustrate this with an example, Figure 5.5 shows an updated version of Kolkata's content density map that only includes content written in each of the three languages. Comparing with Figure 5.3, we see that most of the available content is indeed in English, and that the coverage in Hindi and Bengali is much less dense than initially estimated. Much of the content returned by our crawls for these languages was actually in English.

Building on this observation that local content density can vary widely between languages, we can compare the spatial distribution of these languages. Are certain parts of the city more well-described in some languages than in others?

In monolingual cities, we find that the most widely spoken local language typically has the highest content density across the city. Berlin's

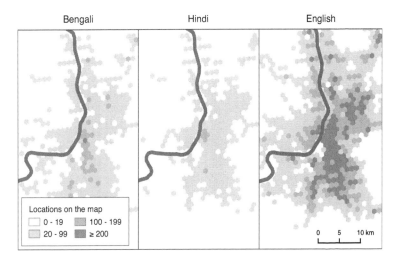

Figure 5.5   Content density in Kolkata for Bengali, English and Hindi. Excluding content that is written in other languages. Data: Google Maps 2019. River features: OpenStreetMap 2020.

map has the most amount of content in German throughout the city (95% of our search locations, the remaining 5% are predominantly English). The same is true in London (predominantly English in 100% of search locations), New York (100% English), São Paulo (100% Portuguese) and Tel Aviv (95% Hebrew). In certain multilingual cities, English-language content dominates the map. English is by far the most prevalent content language across all of Dar es Salaam (99% of search locations), Kolkata (99%), and Nairobi (100%), as we may have expected based on our earlier findings.

However, in other multilingual cities, language distributions can follow intricate spatial patterns. In Brussels, where the volume of French content is almost as high as the content in Flemish, German and English taken together, the French language dominates the representation of the inner city (48% of all search locations), while Flemish content dominates in the suburbs and surrounding region (46% of locations).[3] In downtown Montréal, English and French are both well-represented in the inner city (representing 45% and 55% of all search locations, respectively), however English content tends to be more prevalent in the southern parts of the island of Montreal, and French content tends to be more prevalent in the north.

Hong Kong represents a particularly striking example of such a geolinguistic division (see Figure 5.6). Overall, the Hong Kong map is characterised by a coexistence of English-dominated and Cantonese-dominated areas (44% and 42% of search locations, respectively). Not shown on the map is the marginal presence of predominantly Mandarin-language areas (15%), restricted largely to the periphery. We can see from the map that English is most dominant on the northern coastline of Hong Kong Island and along the downtown coastal promenades, while Cantonese dominates the urban regions of the mainland in Kowloon, and some parts in the north-east side of Hong Kong Island.

Global language geography

From this foundation of having mapped multiple examples of geolinguistic divisions, it is worth exploring the question of language distribution and multilinguality in a more comprehensive manner. We return to the

---

3. Of course, we should remember that while there is more French-language content available about Brussels in principle, we found earlier that English is more commonly used in content substitutions, and is seemingly given preference over other languages.

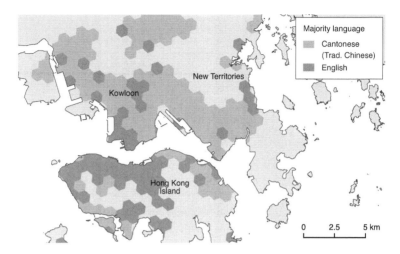

Figure 5.6   Majority content languages in Hong Kong. Indicating where the majority of Google Maps content is in either Cantonese (written in Traditional Chinese script) or English. Data: Google Maps 2019. Coastlines: OpenStreetMap 2020.

global view of the previous chapter, based on a global scan of Google Maps across the world's most widely spoken languages. Which parts of the world are represented in which languages? Which languages are routinely used for content substitutions when content is not available in the original search language? And can we confirm the apparent prevalence of English-language content?

Figure 5.7 shows global coverage maps for four major languages, Arabic, Portuguese, Spanish and French. We can see that content in each of these languages follows a very characteristic distribution, broadly reflecting the global population distributions of these languages; suggesting that Google Maps content is generally available in the languages where they are spoken. Compared to the Arabic- and Spanish-language maps in Figure 4.13, where we include foreign-language content, the actual distribution of content in these languages is much more restricted. (By comparison, the English-language content is broadly unchanged, so we do not show it here.)

These examples are not unique to these languages, rather they are an expression of a general pattern. Figure 5.8 shows that search results across many of the most widely spoken languages will frequently contain foreign-language content – including a significant share of Eng-

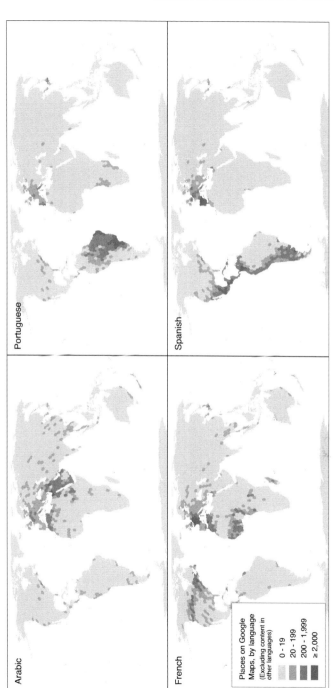

Figure 5.7 Estimated Google Maps coverage in four widely spoken languages: Arabic, Portuguese, French and Spanish. Only including content written in those languages. Data: Google Maps 2019.

lish-language content. (In some cases, such as for Arabic, French and Indonesian, the amount of content returned in English even exceeds the amount returned in the actual search language.) In other words, at this aggregate level we can see that there is a strong overall emphasis on English-language content, which we can see reflected in search results in many other languages.

Interestingly, Figure 5.8 suggests a relatively low incidence of substitution of foreign-language results in Bengali, Hindi and Mandarin Chinese searches. However, rather than indicating that the world is particularly well-described in these languages, it simply reflects a much greater incidence of empty search results for these languages, especially outside their respective home regions. Evidently – and for whatever reason – Google Maps is less likely to attempt foreign-language content substitution for these languages, and is instead more likely to return empty search results.

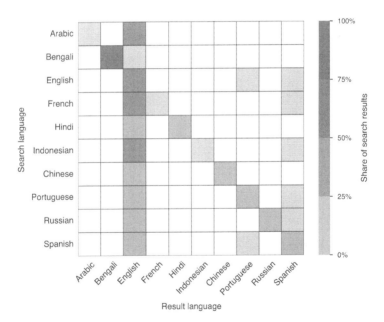

Figure 5.8   Share of search results by search and result language. Darker squares show greater match between search and results language. We can see that English-language content is prevalent in all search results, followed by Spanish; that French, Arabic and Indonesian are often substituted with English content and Bengali rarely; and can also detect a relationship between Spanish and Portuguese. Data: Google Maps 2019.

A GEOLINGUISTIC HEGEMONY?

A large number of unsupported languages?

Despite Google's apparent effort to support a wide range of languages, there are clear differences in content availability between languages. Languages such as the South African Xhosa and Zulu, and the South American Guaraní are almost entirely absent, and cities in which these languages are spoken are instead entirely represented in English, Afrikaans, Spanish and other large languages of the respective regions. This a significant omission: each of the three languages is spoken by millions. Furthermore, their omission prompts us to ask how many of the thousands of active languages in the world are digitally represented on Google Maps.

Even languages that are supported by Google in principle may be less well-supported than might at first appear, and may instead reveal significant content gaps. We see this in the notable example of Swahili, whose speakers are confronted with a peculiar paradox: while user interface elements have been translated into their language, there is very little actual Swahili map content, and speakers of the language need to use English search terms and read English results in order to access Google Maps. Overall, these gaps and omissions confirm our observations of the previous chapter at the local level: map interfaces suggest that underlying data are more diverse than they really are.

Content distributions mirror existing language geographies

Among languages where content is available, we find that the content distribution often appears to follow the social geography of the respective language, as is maybe most strikingly visible for the maps of Arabic, Portuguese, French and Spanish content in Figure 5.7. In practice what this means is that content in languages other than English tends to have distinct regional geographies: something that is hardly surprising – we maybe cannot reasonably expect that Google has translated all content into all languages.

To an extent this is also reflected at the local level. In officially monolingual places like Berlin, São Paulo, New York and Tel Aviv, the official language (German, Brazilian Portuguese, English and Hebrew) is typically the most prevalent language on the map, in terms of both its content density and its prominence in search result listings. But in each of these four cities, maps shown to users are not only restricted to the local majority language, we also see varying amounts of content available in local minority languages, including English.

More striking spatial patterns are evident in cities where multiple official languages coexist: maps of multilingual cities often have some degree of mixed-language content, in spatial distributions that may relate to the cultural geographies of these cities. In Montréal, Brussels, Hong Kong and Kolkata, the respective major local languages are all relatively well-represented, and in several of these cities different languages are associated with different parts of the urban terrain. Once more, English is often among the most content-rich languages in each of these cities, even in Brussels where it is not considered an official language.

Content substitutions seek to address coverage gaps

We have seen many instances of content gaps in a given language being addressed through content substitutions in other languages, leading to search results where multiple languages may coexist. Google likely sees this as desirable because it avoids the appearance of 'blank spots' when information is actually available, particularly in multilingual regions where individuals may be quite comfortable navigating multilingual spaces. For example, French Canadian speakers may not be surprised to find some English-language content on a map of Montréal. This also occurs in other places – often involving content substitutions in English, or in another local language if such content is available.

Yet we also find that such content substitution takes place for some languages more than for others. Notably, Bengali-language searches outside of Bengali-speaking countries yield empty search results rather than foreign-language results. This might be due to the result of a combination of factors involving the social geography of the language, as well as its linguistic features and script that render it comparatively unique among the most widely spoken languages. By contrast, European languages such as English, French, Spanish and Portuguese are linguistically close enough that they may share some common search terms, and languages such as Arabic, Mandarin Chinese, Russian and even Indonesian may be more widely geographically distributed in their everyday use, which means that content in these languages would be more readily available in a larger number of places. Digital content may also simply be more readily available in some languages than others.

An apparent language hegemony

Some of the geolinguistic patterns observed in this chapter are indicators for underlying structural factors that result not merely in digital differences in representation, but in real digital inequality in representation. We can see this in particular in the apparent dominance of English-language content on the platform. Not only is English the most content-rich language on Google Maps, many search results in other languages feature English content, even in places where English would be considered a foreign language. For example, in the map of Brussels we found that during content substitutions, English content was given preference over local languages whenever content was not available in the search language.

In part, this is maybe simply a reflection of the content distribution of Google's geospatial database, which is dominated by English content – and English is one of the most widely spoken languages on the planet. Yet we also need to consider this apparent digital dominance in the context of the various forms of language exclusion we have also observed, including the omission of content in languages with significant populations of speakers. The overall picture that emerges is one where certain languages are amplified, and others are excluded or otherwise marginalised, resulting in a kind of digital hegemony – the dominance of certain languages, and the exclusion of others.

What drives these digital inequalities?

The findings in this chapter confirm observations in the previous chapter at the local level. While many languages and regions are digitally represented in principle, not all are, and many are absent. For certain communities and in certain places, the map is blank. As a result, Google Maps is plainly unusable for many speakers of unsupported languages who have to switch to other languages, including English, in order to navigate the map. These geolinguistic patterns are particularly striking when we look at the multilingual geographies of Brussels, Hong Kong or Kolkata, the geographies of language exclusion in Dar es Salaam and Nairobi, or the digital absences of Zulu, Xhosa and Guaraní. Many of these instances of unequal coverage are inseparable from the social context of these places, and the political and colonial histories of these languages. In such circumstances, digital information gaps can reinforce pre-existing inequalities, particularly when they coincide with other more hegemonic representations.

Although it was not a focus for this chapter, it is worth mentioning that these circumstances can also offer some context for the emergence of mixed-language use and the use of language transliteration in online communication outside of Google Maps, including the use of mixed Arabic–English language forms and the Arabic chat alphabet Arabizi (Warschauer, Said and Zohry 2002; Haggan 2007; El-Essawi 2011), or the stylised digital language variations emerging for Chinese languages (Su 2003; C. Yang 2007). They can be understood as creative expressions of language identity within a new digital medium, as well as necessary responses to the limitations of platforms that cater to certain languages more than others.

We should also emphasise that Google Maps has significantly increased its global coverage since our initial surveys a decade ago, where the digital map was much more sparse outside its initial hotspots of Europe and North America (M. Graham and Zook 2013). Yet even if its coverage steadily improves, Google's map can still only reflect the global realities of the broader information ecologies it depends on. By identifying instances of amplification and exclusion we can start to better understand their potential causes, many of which are external to Google. On the one hand, we are left with an overall impression that Google Maps is in part simply dependent on the content available to it. For example, restaurants may promote themselves in particular languages but not others, and businesses may be more willing or able to promote themselves digitally in some global regions than in others. This is likely further exacerbated by global differences in economic and human development that affect local access to education, information technology and affordable broadband. We will explore many of these factors in the next chapter. In the presence of these and other circumstances, Google Maps can only ever be a mirror of existing social geographies. But it in turn then also enacts versions of these circumstances, based on its presentation of the data that favours some content and some places over others. The outcomes observed here are in part also the result of Google's decision to expand coverage in particular regions and languages but not others, possibly informed by a commercial calculus, such as the presence of a local advertising market.

Overall, we conclude that some of the differences in geographic and linguistic coverage we have identified in Chapter 4 can represent actual digital inequalities, and in some cases even injustice – especially when they are the result of systematic processes of amplification and exclusion that emphasise certain representations at the cost of others. As we have argued in earlier work, the power/knowledge nexus in many of these digital representations is both inherently inclusionary and empowering for some people and places, and inherently exclusionary and disempowering for others (M. Graham and Zook 2013).

But if we seek to better understand how these forms of amplification and exclusion take form, we also need to ask questions about the social, political and informational spheres in which these mappings take place – the presences and absences of geospatial information that feed into digital representations of the world. To explore these driving forces further, in the next chapter we will describe the broader social and economic circumstances that provide a global context for the creation of digital representations. We will then discuss how they can bring about processes of digital participation or exclusion that in turn determine what is shown on our digital maps.

6
Who are the Map-Makers?

Reviewing the geographies of information on Wikipedia and Google Maps has revealed significant inequalities in representation. Indeed, digital representations are often characterised by large content gaps in certain languages and for certain global regions, and coverage is generally greater for regions and languages of the Global North. Representations in a few languages (most notably English) are greatly amplified, while others are not included or marginalised. The end result is a digital hegemony of representation.

The prevalence of these inequalities begs the question to what extent these patterns are driven by an inequality in *participation* – that is, whether this is the simple consequence of an absence of participants from particular regions or language groups. And how voluntary is this absence? Is the production of digital representations inherently inclusive and empowering for some people and places, and inherently exclusionary and disempowering for others?

In this chapter, we want to examine the extent to which digital participation might be a privilege of the few by looking at a broad cross-section of particular forms of digital participation across the world, in an attempt to provide something akin to a basic digital census. Figure 6.1 compares the populations and number of internet users of six world regions with the number of Wikipedia page views and Wikipedia contributions, the number of users of the open-source peer production platform Github, and the median daily users of the anonymisation software Tor. Taken together, they can provide a broad sense of today's global geographies of digital participation.[1]

Figures for population and internet users provide baseline expectations. Africa and Asia taken together represent by far the largest share of the global population. However, compared to these baseline expec-

---

1. Github and Tor are chosen to give an indication of other types of active digital engagement: allowing us to paint a fuller picture of where in the world people are active on platforms that have become internationally dominant in their respective domains.

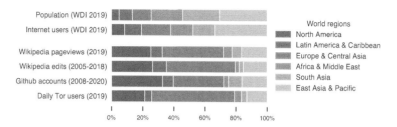

Figure 6.1 Measures of digital participation by world regions. We can see that the Global North is strongly represented in these measures. Data: World Bank 2019, Wikimedia Foundation 2019, Wikipedia 2018, Github 2020, Tor 2019.

tations, our various measures of content production show a markedly different distribution – here, North America and Europe are significantly over-represented across all of these measures, compared to their population sizes.

In other words, the figure shows that the regional inequality in representation we observed in previous chapters reflects a fundamental, regional inequality in digital participation. This echoes a common finding that not all regions in the world participate equally in the social production of digital representation, and that contributions often originate in countries of the Global North (M. Graham, Straumann and Hogan 2015; Sen et al. 2015).

In this chapter we will first consider in more detail *who* in the world gets to participate in the making of digital maps and representations, and then discuss the extent to which some of the peculiarities of digital representation are not simply expressions of global difference, but also the result of an accumulation of multiple processes of social and economic exclusion.

Our inquiry in this chapter is guided by a central question:

- Which regional populations are driving the creation of digital knowledge and representation?

We are particularly interested in aspects that can help us better understand the causes of inequality in representation, including processes by which local participation is either supported or discouraged. We thus elaborate on the question as follows:

- What do the geographic patterns of digital participation look like?

- To what extent are regional inequalities in participation caused by the broader socio-economic environment in which this participation takes place?
- To what extent are participation inequalities caused by platform affordances, and other aspects inherent to the contribution process?

As an entry point into this inquiry, we will first return to Wikipedia as a case study, and consider its participation geography in more detail. We use this as a starting point to investigate the factors that can affect and shape user participation – and thus the capacity to create digital representations – including basic economic considerations such as access to connectivity, and access to leisure time. We then further investigate the role of language and other aspects of our broader information environments that regulate our access to digital information. Finally, we discuss how the design of platforms can present further key barriers to participation. As we will discover in the course of this chapter, many of these factors compound and build on each other.

WHO CONTRIBUTES TO WIKIPEDIA?

As we discussed in Chapter 3, the digital representations of Wikipedia are produced by a global network of thousands of volunteers in a collective process of self-motivated volunteer labour. Who are these people, and where in the world are they located? While in previous chapters we have described geographies of information more broadly, we will now take a closer look at the geography of Wikipedia's contributors.

The demography of social knowledge production

We might expect that Wikipedia's open and participatory approach to knowledge production would result in a highly equitable social arrangement, with participation coming from a broad range of demographics. However, a surprising and much-discussed aspect of Wikipedia's open editing model is its strong participation bias: that is, not all populations participate equally. We see this especially in terms of the platform's gender breakdown. In an early study of highly engaged Wikipedia contributors, only 7 per cent of participants were found to be female (Nov 2007). It was later shown that such a strong gender bias can lead to a topical bias of contributions (Lam et al. 2011). A similar gender divide has been observed for a wide range of other participatory platforms, including both OpenStreetMap and Google MapMaker (Stephens 2013). Across a multitude of surveys, the share of female contributors in Open-StreetMap in particular was found to be as low as 2–5 per cent (Haklay and Budhathoki 2010; Y.-W. Lin 2011; Stark 2011; Lechner 2011; Budhathoki and Haythornthwaite 2013; Neis and Zielstra 2014).

This stark gender divide was likely identified early on because it is relatively easy to observe. By comparison, less information is available about other dimensions of social difference. The first large demographic survey of the Wikipedia community (including both editors and readers) was launched in 2008 by the Wikimedia Foundation and the United Nations University (Glott, Schmidt and Ghosh 2010). Over the course of a few months the survey drew almost 180,000 respondents, most of them participants in the English-, Russian-, Spanish- or German-language editions of Wikipedia. While a full third of respondents stated that they contribute actively to Wikipedia, the remaining two-thirds considered themselves to be readers. Half the survey's respondents were younger than 22 years, possibly reflecting that the Wikipedia project itself was still quite new at the time, having only been launched in 2001. Perhaps corresponding to this relatively young age, around half the respondents stated that secondary education was their highest educational attainment to date, though respondents overall appeared to be well-educated: a quarter had completed an undergraduate degree, and a fifth a graduate or postgraduate degree. The survey also supported the earlier observation of a gender divide: only 13 per cent of respondents were women. This initial Wikipedia survey did not include questions about employment status and economic circumstances, however it is notable that when it asked about reasons not to make a donation to Wikipedia, almost half the respondents stated that they could not afford to make one. When respondents who identified as readers were asked why they did not contribute content, common responses were unfamiliarity with the technology, a lack of knowledge, discomfort editing others' work, concerns about making mistakes, or a lack of time.

While this large-scale survey reflected the particular circumstances of a self-selecting group of active Wikipedians (rather than the population at large), it already offered an early glimpse of the wide spectrum of circumstances that could impede or discourage participation: including the barriers presented by technology interfaces, the prevalent etiquettes and cultural frames around knowledge and authority, and the economic privilege of spare time. We will consider each of these aspects in detail as we examine the possible causes behind diverse forms of exclusion.

Reader geography

One way to estimate the global geography of Wikipedia readers is to look at the Wikipedia traffic that is associated with different world regions. We have already shown a basic aggregate measure of Wikipedia pageviews in Figure 6.1. Building on this, in Figure 6.2 we show a more detailed view of country-level Wikipedia traffic, this time normalised by the size of the local internet population. This map shows where those who are *already* using the internet are more or less likely to also be visiting Wikipedia pages. Overall, the geography of Wikipedia readers is arguably global, but there are also some clear differences in use across regions. Wikipedia is particularly widely used in the Global North, especially North America, Central and Western Europe, and Australia, although other regions are certainly participating as well. We can see from the map that the differences in consumption across regions are surprisingly similar to the inequalities of representation seen in earlier chapters. In particular, many African countries are relatively under-represented in Wikipedia's user base.

These differences in readership are also reflected in markedly different usage patterns. A more recent survey of Wikipedia users by

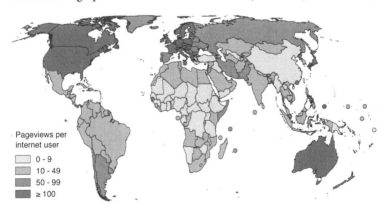

Figure 6.2 Wikipedia pageviews per internet-connected person, across all Wikipedia language versions. Data: Wikimedia Foundation 2019, World Bank 2019.

the Wikimedia Foundation found that reading behaviours in the Global North differed from those in the Global South (Lemmerich et al. 2019). Readers in lower-income countries were found to read articles more in depth, using it as a primary educational resource, while readers in higher-income countries were found to be more likely to search for quick references. Building on this initial finding, a subsequent larger survey was translated to 14 languages across multiple scripts and language families, and almost 70,000 Wikipedia readers responded (Wikimedia 2019). This more detailed survey revealed some striking differences in reader behaviour across language communities and global regions. For example, while the most common self-reported use case for readers of the English, Dutch and Japanese editions is fact-checking and to look up concepts mentioned in media, the most commonly stated use case by readers of languages of the Global South is so-called intrinsic learning, which is the seeking of detailed information and knowledge outside of school or work. Readers of Hindi Wikipedia in particular place a significant focus on in-depth reading. An investigation of Spanish Wikipedia confirmed these seeming differences in usage across global regions, observing that readers from Spanish-speaking countries with a high Human Development Index were less focused on scholarly or technical topics in their browsing behaviour, and instead more interested in media and sports.

In both studies, the survey authors speculate that Wikipedia language editions can be regarded as reflections of the distinct cultural spheres in which they are consumed, and that these results reflect differences in the cultural contexts of Wikipedia use, for example regional differences in Wikipedia's use in education. Importantly, both surveys found that reader behaviour on English Wikipedia is not representative of reader behaviour in other languages, despite some broad commonalities of reader behaviours and use cases. It is further noteworthy that according to the survey data, almost half the readers of the English and French Wikipedias are not native speakers of these languages, which means they are relying on an information resource that exists outside their own culture. As a consequence of these complex social intersections, the authors warn that any averaging of findings or assumptions across language groups likely masks important differences due to the high heterogeneity across groups (Wikimedia 2018; Lemmerich et al. 2019).

This is an eloquent articulation of the basic premise of our book: that the internet is not a global village, that it is instead a rich assemblage of particular communities, all of which partake in distinct and varied interactions with the digital representations that reflect them. These observations help to identify a diversity of readership and use that has not previously been recognised (see also Arora 2019), and they also invite reflection about the diversity of challenges and opportunities experienced by the different Wikipedia language editions, and by other participatory efforts that seek a global reach.

Contributor geography

Although Wikipedia makes much of its data publicly available, for privacy reasons location information about registered contributors is not made public. However, the geography of contributors can nevertheless be approximated based on information recorded in the contribution history. Anonymous edits on Wikipedia by contributors who have *not* registered an account are associated with an IP address, and this information is recorded and publicly available.[2] Many such IP addresses are resolvable to a broad geographic location, and we can look up these geographies at country resolution using publicly available Geo-IP databases. While this does not allow for a reliable estimate of editor numbers, the information can be used to observe the relative volume of contribution flows coming from particular regions. The resulting estimate of Wikipedia's contribution geography offers a best-effort measure that has been shown to closely reflect the actual contribution geography (M. Graham, Straumann and Hogan 2015).

Figure 6.3 visualises this global contributor geography, that is, the number of anonymous edits originating in each country, normalised by the country's internet population. The map is striking in its similarity to the reader geography we showed in Figure 6.2. We can see that overall, the contributor geography is heavily dominated by the Global North, in particular North America and Europe. Editors from these countries contribute at least an order of magnitude more than people from other global regions. As discussed, this closely mirrors the representation geographies presented in previous chapters. Taken together they demonstrate the close link between processes of participation and representation: the same global regions that provide most of the contributions also benefit from the most detailed representations on Wikipedia.

2. Approximately 20% of edits are made by unregistered users (or users who have chosen not to log in).

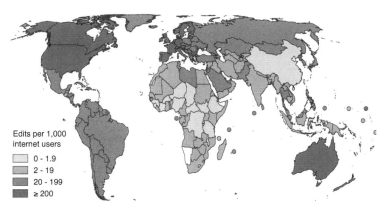

Figure 6.3 Anonymous Wikipedia edits across all language versions by contributor location, normalised by the number of internet users in each country. Data: Wikipedia 2018, World Bank 2019.

This spatial distribution however is dependent on which part of Wikipedia we are looking at. Figure 6.4 shows that contributor distributions vary significantly by Wikipedia language edition, and often seem to follow the population distribution of the respective language. English Wikipedia is by far the most active, and its distribution is similar to the overall one in Figure 6.3. By comparison, the smaller Spanish Wikipedia is largely produced in South-West Europe and Latin America; the Arabic Wikipedia in the Middle East and North Africa; and the Hindi Wikipedia in South and West Asia, along with North America and a few other

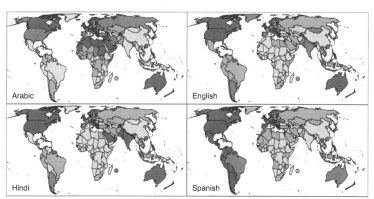

Figure 6.4 Edits to the Arabic-, English-, Hindi- and Spanish-language editions of Wikipedia. Normalised by the number of internet users in each country, and segmented in quartiles (four parts of equal size). Data: Wikipedia 2018, World Bank 2019.

countries. (We will look at this question of local-language geography in more detail in the next chapter.)

Figure 6.5 allows us to place these regional activities in proportion. How much editing activity originates in the different regions of the world, and how does it shift over time? We can see that most of Wikipedia's contributions originate in Europe, North America and East Asia. Contributions from Europe and North America have stagnated in recent years, possibly a saturation effect, as much content is already available in the major languages of these regions. By comparison, the volume of contributions from the African and South Asian regions has historically been around 5 per cent of the volume of edits coming from Europe, and Latin American countries have contributed about a fifth. And yet, the figure also shows there is apparent (if slight) growth in contribution activity from these regions.

To put this recent growth in perspective, Figure 6.6 shows the contribution volumes from these regions as a proportion of European contributions. The chart illustrates that the relative proportion of contributions from African and South Asian editors in particular has grown in recent years. In the decade between 2007 and 2017, the share of contributions from Africa and South Asia has more than doubled, and the chart shows that the growth rates of these regions now exceed that of

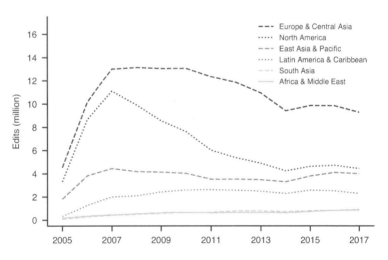

Figure 6.5 Wikipedia edits by anonymous editors over time, by editor location, across all Wikipedia language versions. Data: Wikipedia 2018.

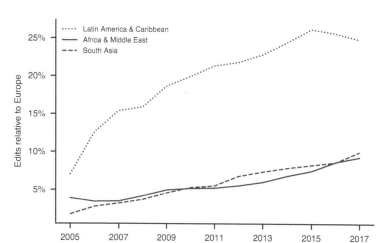

Figure 6.6 Wikipedia edits by editor location relative to Europe, across all Wikipedia language versions. Data: Wikipedia 2018.

Europe. Yet, contributors located in Europe are still producing a multiple of the Wikipedia content volumes of other global regions.

INFORMATION ENVIRONMENTS

To better understand what drives these global inequalities in representation and participation we will review the key causal factors that have been proposed by academics and policy-makers over the years. This includes factors at both the macro- and micro-scales, that is, including both the broader economic and cultural contexts that support or impede digital participation across a region, and the individual experiences of digital participants.

Broadband connectivity

Any inquiry into the drivers and barriers of digital participation needs to start by confronting a basic fact: global connectivity is unequally distributed. Today this more often relates to the basic *cost* of connectivity rather than the limits of the physical information networks, such as speed or coverage. A recent ICANN report on the digital economy in the Middle East and North Africa observes: 'For many people in the region, connectivity is either unavailable or unaffordable' (Dean 2017). The report argues that as a result the region is characterised by a digital divide, where internet access is limited to an economically privileged subset of the population. Here, as in other parts of the world, the cost of basic connectivity presents the first barrier to participation.

Figure 6.7 shows a population-normalised map of internet users as a proportion of the national population, based on 2019 data by the World Bank. As with many of the maps we have reviewed so far, the map reveals the striking presence of the Global North: almost all the countries with an internet penetration rate above 75 per cent are to be found in Europe or North America. But in absolute terms, China now represents the largest population of internet users, and India one of the largest. In other words, in some of the world's largest nations there is still substantial room for digital growth. For example, more than half of all African countries only have an internet penetration of under 25 per cent, and in many other countries of the Global South (including, for example, Pakistan, India and Myanmar) internet penetration is still below 50 per cent.

It may be surprising to readers of the Global North that the relatively high cost of broadband is a clear central driver behind such absences. In certain regions of the world, a broadband connection can cost more than the average monthly wage. Figure 6.8 visualises the results of a global market survey by the International Telecommunications Union, relating the cost of an entry-level fixed home broadband connection to average earnings (ITU 2017). This map is an almost perfect inversion of the internet-users map of Figure 6.7, and together they tell a clear

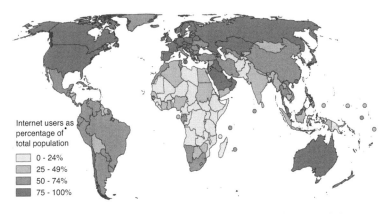

Figure 6.7 Internet users per country as share of the population. Includes internet use via computer, mobile device, gaming device, digital TV, on so on. Data: World Bank 2019.

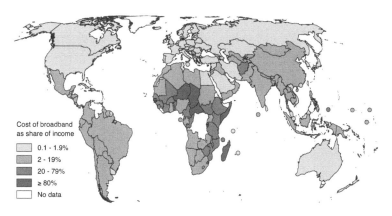

Figure 6.8 Cost of broadband relative to average income. Data: ITU 2017.

story: internet adoption is lowest in places where connectivity is most expensive. In particular, many communities in Africa and the broader Global South are confronted with a prohibitively high cost for internet access in proportion to their earnings. At the same time, the last decade has seen an expansion of global fibre networks and related infrastructure development, resulting in lower cost and incredible growth of global connectivity, particularly on the African continent and in the Global South (ITU 2017). As a result, the distributions shown here are already less unequal than in our earliest reports on this issue (M. Graham et al. 2014; M. Graham, De Sabbata and Zook 2015).

Does growth in global connectivity afford a greater capacity for self-representation by local communities? Our early investigations of this question have revealed that the relationship between connectivity and participation in Wikipedia is complicated, and that in many regions of the Global South, availability of internet connectivity alone does not result in a proportional increase in online participation: that is, not all regions respond to improved connectivity in the same way (M. Graham et al. 2014). This is accompanied by an apparent threshold effect. In a 2015 study we found that connectivity improvements drive Wikipedia participation rates only in countries that are already participating significantly (M. Graham, Straumann and Hogan 2015). In response to this finding, we speculate that digital participation may become more attractive when there are already digital resources available in one's own language that relate to the interests and needs of one's own community. However, the real relationships are doubtlessly more nuanced.

Overall, it can be said that efforts to improve connectivity in Africa and elsewhere have led to mixed outcomes, particularly in lower-income countries, which suggests that connectivity alone is insufficient to foster digital participation, and that there are additional factors that inform the decision to participate (Friederici, Ojanperä and Graham 2017). We will consider these in the remainder of the chapter.

Participation as labour

Building further on these observations around economic circumstance we want to propose a second key driver of participation and exclusion: the fact that the capacity to engage in volunteer labour is not equally distributed. Our argument is twofold: contributing to digital knowledge production is a highly skilled activity, and consequently it needs to be recognised as a form of unpaid labour.

It has perhaps become clear from our discussion so far that participation in social knowledge production is a specialist practice that requires knowledge of particular processes and technologies. An example of this is the contribution norms and other specialist procedures involved in social knowledge production on Wikipedia – or indeed on OpenStreetMap, where contribution requires specialist tools and an understanding of specialist concepts (Graham, Straumann and Hogan 2015; Sen et al. 2015). Overall, it is not a stretch to consider participation in social knowledge production to be a form of specialist labour. While it is largely unpaid labour, we can nevertheless consider the diverse forms of paid labour behind Google Maps and other commercial platforms to get a sense of the relative value of the resulting digital representations – we refer back to our discussions of Google's digital supply chain in Chapter 3.

With this in mind, we should note the high levels of subsistence labour worldwide, which strongly limits the capacity for voluntary or uncompensated participation in many parts of the world. To illustrate this second aspect, we again refer to the Human Development Index, which encapsulates a number of diverse economic and social measures: per capita income, education levels and life expectancy. As we have seen earlier in this chapter, the index is highly correlated with a capacity to engage in digital volunteering: countries ranking high on the index also have higher participation rates in digital knowledge production. We can also describe global economic circumstances in terms of distribution of global wealth: according to the 2015 CreditSuisse Global Wealth Report,

North America represents less than 20 per cent of the global population, but more than 65 per cent of the global wealth (Shorrocks, Davies and Lluberas 2015). According to the report, the richest people in the world live in the US, China, the UK, Germany, Switzerland and other countries of the Global North. A gradual shift in income is reducing these wealth inequalities over time as more people join a growing global middle class, largely driven by continued economic growth in China and to a lesser extent in India. But 70 per cent of the world's adult population still has a net worth below USD \$10,000, with no expectation to reach middle class prosperity any time soon – most of them living outside North America and Europe. Again, these distributions resemble the maps of digital representation and participation that we have reviewed so far.

In this context, it matters that participation in Wikipedia is primarily conceived as a volunteering model. This is a strong element of its collective identity; the idea that a global community can capture the world's knowledge in a collective process that is driven by people's passion for knowledge rather than profit-seeking. Wikipedia's reluctance to pay contributors is partly also an attempt to reduce conflicts of interest, and to keep lobbying and advertising efforts off the platform. These are understandable concerns. And yet, we have to recognise that this model of self-selecting volunteers works well in contexts where contributors feel sufficiently rewarded by the experience – we refer back to our discussion of the motivational drivers of Wikipedia participation in Chapter 3. People commonly contribute to Wikipedia because it improves their experience of their own lives, because it is enjoyable to do so, and because they believe that the information contained in Wikipedia should be free. But not everyone around the world enjoys the economic conditions that allow them to spend time writing on Wikipedia, and differences in economic circumstances can drastically alter someone's capacity and motivation to take part in online knowledge production. Instead, it is increasingly clear that the volunteering model is not necessarily a good match for actual global circumstance.

Is the reluctance to pay editors a barrier to equitable participation on Wikipedia? Not exactly. Global economic inequalities mean that an encyclopaedia built on paid edits would also reflect those inequalities. We'd probably have an encyclopaedia with even more content about rich countries and wealthy corporations than we already do. What we instead need are models that both address the fact that different parts of the world have different capacities to volunteer, and at the same time remove some of the short-term problematic incentives that paid editing would bring about.

One such model is the Wikipedian in residence, a paid position to work within a cultural or educational institution and help them contribute their knowledge to Wikipedia. In these cases, the contributed knowledge has often already been vetted by the institution, and the Wikipedian in residence can be considered more a facilitator than an author of original writing.

Information ecologies

Once the basic barriers of connectivity and availability of spare time have been addressed, further basic prerequisites to participation relate to the broader information environment. Participation in digital knowledge production requires access to forms of knowledge and information – acquired for example through formal education or disseminated by local media and publishers. Literacy itself is obviously a necessary and basic precondition for digital participation. This also includes digital literacy, for example the ability to critically evaluate sources, to locate the relevant contribution policies, to access and include references that provide substantiation for any claims made, and the capacity to learn wiki syntax (M. Graham and Hogan 2014). These factors further illustrate why the Human Development Index is such a good predictor for digital participation. (Of course, such capacities and forms of support can also be absent among participants in comparatively wealthy societies.)

One significant barrier to global digital participation is a frequent lack of secondary information sources. Wikipedia aims to aggregate and summarise external sources, rather than be a publishing platform for original writing or information. Consequently, Wikipedia articles rely on references to public reporting in media, academic publishing and open access government documents, all of which need to be available in order to be able to produce Wikipedia content. Yet, the global production and availability of these is highly unequal (M. Graham and Hogan 2014). As a consequence, the relative health of a local media environment will impact the local capacity to produce Wikipedia content. In one study of a sample of English Wikipedia articles, 80 per cent of publishers of cited source material were located in a country whose primary language is English (Ford et al. 2013). This finding has been reproduced for other Wikipedia languages (Sen et al. 2015). These information ecologies are impactful even beyond social knowledge production: it has been shown that a well-developed local publishing sector can markedly improve the representation of cities in search engine results (Ballatore, Graham and Sen 2017).

A shared language can be an important further enabler, as illustrated by the Wikipedia readership surveys we discussed earlier in this chapter. Language is an important catalyst of social encounter, and thus certain global language communities can draw from a larger pool of potential participants. Sometimes this can extend to communities of related or neighbouring languages – it has been shown that participants contributing to multiple Wikipedia language editions are motivated to do so because they are either bilingual, or able to speak a language that is similar enough to make a contribution possible (Karimi et al. 2015; Samoilenko et al. 2016). Less important motivational factors for participating in other language editions were a shared religion (a possible proxy for a shared cultural environment), and geographic proximity with the target community. The combination of these factors constitutes a kind of linguistic neighbourhood which in turn becomes an enabler for shared contribution efforts (Samoilenko ct al. 2016).

Similar linguistic neighbourhoods exist in media reporting and news consumption, where they are significantly shaped by cultural and geographic context. A study of the national media landscapes across 193 countries found identifiable information flows between countries, often tied to geographic, linguistic, historical, or cultural similarities (Hill 2013). Such information ties have been identified between Brazil, Argentina and Paraguay, and between Croatia, Bosnia and Herzegovina and Serbia. However, such ties are not always reciprocated. For example, the Algerian public pays significant attention to coverage about France and the US, and the French public to coverage of the US, while the US public doesn't pay significant attention to media coverage of either of these countries. But overall, news consumption is always most strongly focused on local and regional issues (Kwak et al. 2018).

PARTICIPATION ENVIRONMENTS

Platform design is another important factor that informs digital participation. This is only partly a matter of user interface design, and is as much about the participation processes and social environments brought about by the platform. Research in fields such as Human–Computer Interaction and Social Computing can help us understand these processes.

Platform norms and affordances

Important participation barriers can emerge from a platform's accepted standards of behaviour, such as its social norms or its quality requirements for contributions. In some cases, such norms are inherent in the fundamental design of a platform, for example as values that underlie the shared activity, and in others they emerge over time, for example in the form of new rules of conduct that help manage growth. For Wikipedia, maybe the most important design choice was the decision to use the form of an encyclopaedia as its foundational model of knowledge production. The encyclopaedia is a specific form of knowledge representation that is rooted in a particular cultural and historic context. As a consequence of this design choice, many of Wikipedia's core policies are derived from an understanding of what an encyclopaedia is – such as its use of a neutral voice and adoption of a neutral point of view, its prohibition of original research, and its reliance on external references as sources of authority (Hill 2013).

Wikipedia policies have necessarily become more complex as the platform has matured, and now increasingly present unexpected barriers to newcomers who need to become familiar with the intricacies of Wikipedia contribution culture (Halfaker et al. 2013). Of course, the encyclopaedic norms were already barriers to contributors from environments where secondary sources are unavailable (M. Graham and Hogan 2014), or where oral and other forms of knowledge need to be transcribed into written (and published) form before they can be captured (Pentzold 2009). As a result, cultures where knowledge and information are not traditionally captured in a formal written form are presented with a fundamental epistemic barrier: the knowledge always needs to be translated into a particular encyclopaedic form.

These particular platform norms introduce contribution barriers in an effort to control and manage contribution flows. However, the assumptions behind these norms are not always made explicit, and the global implications are not always reflected on. These norms can yield outcomes that are in perfect agreement with codified contribution policies, but that arguably contravene the intended purpose of collective and global knowledge production. For example, Wikipedia coverage of major floods in low-income and non-English speaking countries is often fragmented or non-existent specifically due to a lack of citable sources, resulting in a situation where such articles are limited to perspectives by Western media that reinforce stereotypes or provide an otherwise superficial representation (Lorini et al. 2020).

Such outcomes illustrate the significant challenge of trying to create global policy for a global project when this is approached from the vantage point of a particular culture, and when cultural assumptions are consequently embedded in interface design. This can extend far beyond the limits of citation practice and can involve expectations of prior knowledge, expectations of etiquette and forms of interaction, or even foundational beliefs, all of which vary quite significantly between global cultures (Kyriakoullis and Zaphiris 2016). In general, platform designers do not always consider to what extent their decisions are informed by their particular cultural context, and whether certain practices and circumstances can be considered to be globally universal.

Further platform barriers arise in the design of user interfaces, where catering to global audiences can present many unexpected challenges. The most immediate challenge is the translation of interface elements into other languages, but designers are presented with many more dimensions of complexity, including layout adaptation for right-to-left languages, providing support for non-Western writing systems and scripts, and even the provision of suitable fonts, all of which are not always considered from the start. For example, Arabic Wikipedia has in the past used fonts that many speakers of the language consider to be difficult to read (M. Graham and Hogan 2014). Some of these aspects may seem like surface issues that are easily addressed, but in practice culturally appropriate and supportive interface design requires deep contextual understanding.

At a more basic level, even the technologies required for platform development embed their own cultural assumptions. Most notably, the tools and programming languages used to develop platforms often assume a deep familiarity with English. As a result, software developers who are well-placed to build technologies for particular global cultures but who are not suitably fluent in English may be unable to do so. It can be argued that the development of new technology is often more challenging for people who are not native English speakers, and who do not have access to an education that helps them become suitably fluent in the language, which thus further limits the spectrum of cultural perspectives that are represented in platform designs (McCulloch 2019).

Platforms as social spheres

Participation in social knowledge production is a specialist practice, a form of labour, that requires knowledge of specialist processes, technologies and contribution norms. It can thus be said that participation in digital knowledge production requires *socialisation*: it requires training, the development of new skills and the formation and maintenance of relationships with the contributor community. And yet, contributions are typically made by volunteers who contribute by choice, rather than through monetary incentive – contributors participate in social knowledge production because they enjoy the process, and because they feel that the experience improves their lives.

As a consequence of this focus on volunteer labour, platform designers are confronted with a fundamental trade-off: to design tasks that will elicit valuable contributions while maintaining the interest of the available volunteers. A contribution experience that introduces unexpected complexity, or that frustrates participants in other ways, can be a deterrent for participation (Wiggins and Crowston 2011). Conversely, it has been found that the provision of a supportive social environment for new contributors can significantly improve newcomer retention, be it through the provision of feedback and mentoring, through problem-solving support, or through the provision of a shared social experience (Haklay and Weber 2008; Dittus, Quattrone and Capra 2016b; Dittus and Capra 2017). For example, evaluation studies of Wikipedia socialisation practices have found that early user retention could be increased by the use of welcome messages, assistance and constructive criticism (Choi et al. 2010; Ciampaglia and Taraborelli 2015).

In these ways, social interactions are often a foundational part of the overall participation experience that provide important motivators for continued engagement. A welcoming social environment can be more than a source of support, it can also be an attractor, and the presence of a community of practice can significantly affect a person's willingness to contribute (Schervish and Havens 1997). Social interactions in digital spaces can provide important sources of individual and collective purpose, particularly in heterogeneous and dispersed volunteer groups (Koh et al. 2007). However, social arrangements can also lead to adverse effects, for example when community members act as gate-keepers in ways that reinforce existing group imbalances such as gender biases (Stephens 2013). In the context of social knowledge production, further adverse effects arise in the form of content disputes and other conflicts between contributors (Kittur et al. 2007; Sumi and Yasseri 2011; Yasseri et al. 2012). In such moments of interpersonal or group conflict, a platform's capacity to identify and respond to targeted harassment and other forms of violence can become a deciding factor in a participant's decision to remain engaged. Respondents to an anti-harassment survey on Wikipedia stated that many issues they had reported to moderators were handled well, yet the overall perception was that personal attacks and long-term disputes between individuals are often handled poorly (Sinders, Poore and Earley 2018). Multiple studies have documented that such unaddressed violence on the internet can become a strong motivator to abandon participation, particularly when they involve indi-vidualised attacks (Reagle 2012; Konieczny 2018; Raish 2019).

In considering these varied social effects it would be a mistake to regard platforms as mere assemblages of technical infrastructure and organisational procedures. Rather, we also need to understand platforms as collective arrangements of people, and as shared spaces for social inter-action. Digital platforms are spaces for communities, scenes and cliques, and as a result they are at the same time both porous and hermetic – they offer social attractors as well as social barriers, and some of the resulting social interactions can manifest as unexpected forms of social exclusion. In these moments it can matter deeply whether platform procedures are able to account for cultural difference, rather than relying on unreflex-ive assumptions that are informed by a particular cultural environment.

LIMITS TO THE UNIVERSAL PLATFORM?

In response to our opening questions about Wikipedia's participation geography, we can say that not all participating groups are equally repre-sented in the creation of digital representations. Instead, both readership and contribution flows are strongly characterised by participation of communities from the Global North, especially North America, Europe and certain parts of Asia, while many other parts of the world are much less actively involved – notwithstanding signs of recent growth. This unequal distribution of participation very closely reflects the representation inequalities discussed in previous chapters: a small number of editors in a small number of countries are responsible for the majority of all contributions.

To its great credit, the Wikipedia community has taken on these concerns with great seriousness. Since the first reports of participation inequalities, hundreds of Wikipedia projects have launched to address systemic bias on the platform, spanning concerns such as the prevalent and ongoing gender bias, and underrepresentation of particular geographic regions and particular communities (Wikipedia 2021b). In a 2017 strategy document, the Wikimedia Foundation first articulated the strategic goal of 'knowledge equity', a concerted effort to counteract structural inequalities and to ensure a just representation of knowledge and people in the Wikimedia movement (Wikimedia 2017). In addition, countless small and large initiatives outside the formal structures of Wikipedia are contributing their efforts towards more equitable representation on Wikipedia. This includes larger efforts such as Visible Wiki Women and Decolonizing the Internet which are organised by the global campaign group Whose Knowledge? (Wikimedia 2021), as well as innumerable smaller events around the world that assist newcomers to fill existing knowledge gaps on the platform (Wikipedia 2021a).

Yet, while such initiatives seek to address existing inequalities within the platform, it is important to acknowledge that the underlying drivers are often external. In trying to explain these inequalities we have identified key participation barriers that relate to the lived circumstances of particular global communities. Many communities are still excluded from participation by the cost of broadband: in certain regions of the world, a broadband connection can cost more than the average monthly wage. However, broadband access itself is not a guarantee for participation, and not all regions respond to increased connectivity in the same way. We have further argued that participation inequalities relate to the vast differences in global wealth which strongly limit many people's capacity for uncompensated labour, especially when considering that social knowledge production is a specialist practice that requires not just spare time, but often also training and experience. As a result, the basic volunteering model of social knowledge production may present a fundamental impediment to equitable and global participation.

Norms and affordances of participatory platforms can present additional significant barriers to participation, especially when they are informed by assumptions that originate in particular cultural environments and that may not be globally universal. This includes platform policies that seek to codify a platform's standards of acceptable contributions. For example, Wikipedia's choice of the encyclopaedia as its fundamental model is rooted in a particular cultural and historic context, and it seeks to represent knowledge in particular ways. Notably, it relies on a supportive information ecology such as a scholarly environment and media sources that can be cited as secondary sources. As a consequence, coverage of topics in low-income and non-English-speaking countries is often fragmented or non-existent due to a lack of citable local sources, resulting in a situation where articles skew to perspectives by Western media that reinforce stereotypes or provide an otherwise superficial representation. These outcomes are in perfect agreement with codified contribution policies, but they arguably contravene the intended purpose of collective and global knowledge production. Further participation barriers may be embedded in the interface design, such as a lack of support for particular languages and scripts, or may relate to the social interactions taking place on the platform, such as the lack of a supportive social environment, or unaddressed issues regarding disputes and harassment.

Yet it would be insufficient to simply regard the question of unequal participation as a matter of having to catch up with the Global North. Rather than projecting the absence of any agency on prospective participants we also have to consider whether these technologies and platforms are in fact universally appealing or even appropriate, especially considering that they are often designed in very particular cultural environments. The assumptions about the world and how it can be represented through maps found in universalist mapping projects are not compatible with the range of ways humans experience and understand space (Winichakul 1994; Steinauer-Scudder 2018).

We should therefore also reflect on the limits of universalist technologies, and we need to consider the possibility that an absence of participation might be a simple matter of deliberate choice – that is, a conscious opting out.[3]

We especially need to bear in mind the central observation in this chapter; that we are looking not at a singular group of connected participants, but at a rich assemblage of communities and cultural spheres, all

3. There are numerous examples of communities choosing to opt out of universalist mapping projects (see Wainwright 2013).

of which are participating in distinct and varied interactions with each other. This is quite a different and more complex arrangement than the utopian expectations of the early internet pioneers, who imagined the internet as one large global community. Instead, we now understand that we need to look much more closely at how different communities are engaging with digital representations. This is also a question of representativeness. Are the digital representations of the world today largely produced by a small and privileged minority, or do they also allow for the self-representation of communities that are marginalised, or that experience other forms of social and political oppression? We will look at the interactions between particular communities in more detail in the next chapter, with a particular focus on the tensions that can arise in the process of creating digital representations. We will also investigate the extent to which digital representations can successfully support a collective capacity for self-representation.

7

Information Power and Inequality

Having observed significant inequalities in digital representations of place, and having looked at the ways in which they are shaped by processes of digital participation and exclusion, we will now bring these elements into conversation with one another. Given that many of the world's populations are presented with significant barriers of access, we thus want to interrogate who creates and has access to digital representations, and how equitable the mechanisms are which are producing them.

In other words, we want to look more closely at how different populations are engaging with digital representations of the world today. Who owns, controls and shapes these augmented and hybrid digital/physical layers of place? Who gets to represent whom?

- Which populations get to shape and access digital representations of the world?

Picking up from our participation analysis in Chapter 6, we first look at the interconnections between contributors of content and represented place in more detail, devoting particular attention to the varied relationships enacted by particular populations. What are the dominant groups that are shaping certain digital representations of the world, and what is their impact on final outcomes? To what extent is local content written by outsiders, rather than local contributors who are familiar with the spaces they are mapping?

We then look more closely at what happens when tensions emerge between participating groups. We will identify instances of digital representations of the world that are contested, and observe how they play out in practice. This includes territorial disputes in the Middle East and other parts of the world which pre-date popular digital representation, but which have now acquired a digital afterlife, as well as more recent neighbourhood-naming disputes in the wake of a high-pressure San Francisco property market, and other examples.

Ultimately this chapter looks at the dominant narrators emerging in the world's contested representations, and considers examples of the struggle of minority groups to contest the perspectives of powerful outsiders. We find that the map-making process is an act of representation in the fullest sense: it constructs spatial realities, and we find that in moments of contestation certain perspectives tend to prevail. As we will see, many of the tensions emerging around digital representation are thus inextricably interwoven with questions of political power and political history, and we will illustrate this with examples of contested representations and misrepresentations across a range of digital platforms. However, we are not just interested in simple disputes or interpersonal disagreement. Rather, we are looking for arrangements where platforms become complicit parties in the negotiations between multiple groups of actors, and we want to then ask which positions they take – implicitly or explicitly.

WIKIPEDIA'S GEOLINGUISTIC CONTOURS

In the previous chapter we identified multiple barriers that can result in inequalities of digital participation. One immediate effect of this unequal participation has been known for some time: digital content about some parts of the world is rarely produced in those places.

As a starting point for our inquiry, we want to explore this issue in more detail, with a focus on local knowledge production and local knowledge access on Wikipedia.

Who produces local representations?

We first want to look at Wikipedia's participation geography with some more specificity: which populations are writing about which places? Most importantly, to what extent are digital representations of certain countries in the world produced by people from the respective country? The map in Figure 7.1 visualises the degree to which articles about particular countries in the world have been written by people from these countries, using data on Wikipedia's contributor geography that we presented in the previous chapter. We consider this to be a map of local content equity: the capacity of a place to tell its own stories, and to produce its own representations.

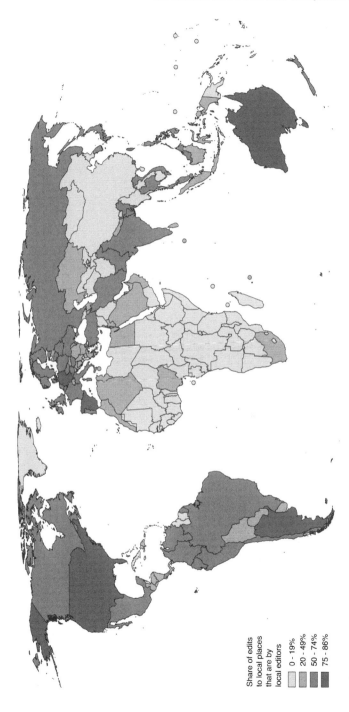

Share of edits
to local places
that are by
local editors

0 - 19%
20 - 49%
50 - 74%
75 - 86%

Figure 7.1 Wikipedia's local content equity. The map shows the share of contributions to local places that are by local editors, among all contributions to local places, across all Wikipedia language versions. Data: Wikipedia 2018.

The map shows quite a striking inequality of authorship: Wikipedia representations of many African and Asian countries are largely written by outsiders. Indeed, the representations of many African countries appear to be largely externally produced, including countries with widespread broadband access such as South Africa (only 35% of edits come from within the country), Kenya (20% of edits) and Namibia (under 10%). On average, less than 15 per cent of contributions about African countries are produced from within those countries, compared to 40 per cent in Europe and South Asia, 25 per cent in East Asia and the Pacific region, and 30 per cent in Latin America. By comparison, countries in North America are largely the authors of their own representations, where on average almost half of all edits are from within. Globally the US leads with 85 per cent, followed by Taiwan, Germany, Australia and Argentina, each of which produce around 80 per cent of their own representations.

To provide a more comprehensive picture, the individual contribution flows across global regions are visualised in Figure 7.2 (outflows) and

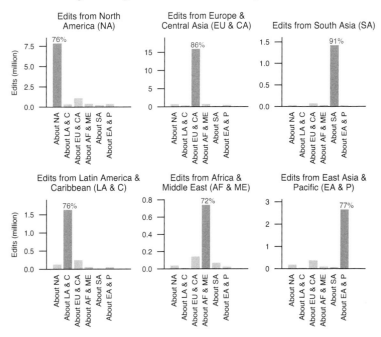

Figure 7.2 Contribution outflows on Wikipedia per global region. The graphs indicate where in the world people from a particular region are writing about. Measured in millions of contributions (edits) by anonymous editors, across all Wikipedia language versions. Data: Wikipedia 2018.

Figure 7.3 (inflows). Figure 7.2 shows contribution outflows per region; that is, the flow of contributions by editors that originate *within* a particular region. The figure further breaks down which regions are being represented by their contributions. We can see that for all regions, the main focus is to represent oneself. Depending on the region, between 70 and 90 per cent of all edits about a place are representations of one's own region, or what we might call self-representations. The remaining minority share of 10–30 per cent of edits is spent on representations outside the contributor's own region, or what we might call outsider representations. This is true for contributor communities around the world, at least when seen from this highly aggregated perspective where we combine the behaviours of thousands or even millions of people per region.

In contrast, Figure 7.3 visualises the contribution inflows per global region. These are the representations that are being produced *about* each region, further broken down by where these representations origi-

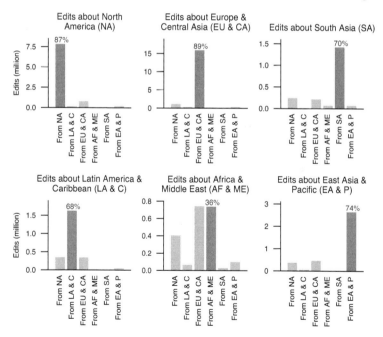

Figure 7.3   Contribution inflows on Wikipedia per global region. The graphs indicate where in the world content about a particular region originated. Measured in millions of contributions (edits) by anonymous editors, across all Wikipedia language versions. Data: Wikipedia 2018.

nated. This allows us to compare the proportions of self-representation and outsider representation for each region. Here it becomes apparent that in addition to local representation efforts, many regions are also receiving large numbers of outside contributions. Africa presents a particularly striking instance of this, where the total volume of outsider contributions is twice as big as all contributions from within, and where European contributions alone equal those originating locally (each accounting for 35% of all incoming edits). To an extent, Latin America and the Caribbean, East Asia and the Pacific and South Asia are also subject to a slightly higher degree of outsider representation, however their contribution capacity appears to be closer to that of North America and Europe, where 90 per cent of all incoming contributions come from within the respective region.

In other words, Wikipedia representations of Africa and the Middle East are to a significant degree written by contributors in Europe and North America. These proportions help explain how the global content equity distribution of Figure 7.1 has come about: although Wikipedia's participation base is arguably global, certain regions of the world are faced with more contributions coming from outside than from within. These forms of outsider representation are not a problem in themselves. However, as we shall see later in this chapter, in the context of differing perspectives and disagreements, such unequal relationships can affect a smaller community's capacity for self-representation.

We should also emphasise that this is not simply the effect of a North–South divide; rather, such imbalanced contributions can be found in many different places, including in the Global North. In Central Europe, Germany in particular has significant outflows to its closest neighbours. German editors contributed more than 10 per cent of all edits to pages about Poland across all languages, almost 15 per cent of edits about Czechia, and 20 per cent of all edits about Austria. A similar relationship can be seen in Russia's contributions to the Ukraine (10% of edits), the UK's to Pakistan (almost 15%), and others. A particularly extreme case is China, which is largely absent as a Wikipedia participant, and as a result is mostly written about from the outside: by editors in the US (20% of edits), followed by Japan, Hong Kong and Germany (each around 5% of edits), and others. The reasons for these uneven relationships are naturally contingent to each region. Each case could warrant its own chapter-length treatment into the ways that colonial histories, patterns of migration, state-led geopolitical conflicts and myriad other factors produce the inequities in the ways places are represented from abroad. Our purpose here, rather, is to simply show that these broad geographic patterns exist.

To put these contribution imbalances in perspective, Figure 7.4 shows growing local participation across all regions, including populations that were previously under-represented. Increasingly, participating populations contribute local knowledge to local representations, indicating a shift towards self-representation. We can see that Europe, North America and the East Asia and the Pacific region have had high degrees of self-representation throughout Wikipedia's history. In contrast, early representations of South Asia, Latin America and Africa were largely written by outsiders. This was likely also a result of Wikipedia's early participation inequality: there were orders of magnitude more participants from outside these regions than within. Yet more recently, the capacity for self-representations in each of these regions has grown immensely. This trend has been particularly dramatic in South Asia and Latin America, which each more than doubled their share of contributions to local representations, and which are now on par with North America and Europe. In Africa, where the initial contribution share was lowest, and where the shift has been less rapid, capacity to self-represent has already doubled, and an end to local capacity growth is not yet in sight. This is in part the

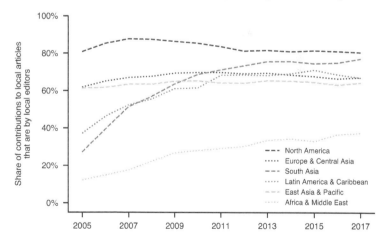

Figure 7.4 Local content equity on Wikipedia over time. Showing the share of Wikipedia contributions to local places that are by local editors, as a proportion of all contributions for each region, across all Wikipedia languages. Data: Wikipedia 2018.

result of regional efforts: in Africa we saw that on average only around 15 per cent of edits come from within a country (Figure 7.1), but looking at Africa as a whole, more than 30 per cent of edits originate from within the region (Figure 7.3). These regional edits are in themselves not necessarily an indicator of greater self-representation, however we do see patterns of an emerging regional localism.[1]

Who has access to local-language representations?

Chapter 5 looked at the question of local-language content in a series of case studies. It showed that some local languages are not well-represented on the platform, even if they are spoken by millions. Building on this finding, we now seek to build a more comprehensive understanding of the matter of local-language access on Wikipedia. This time we are not limited to a small number of regional case studies, as we have access to all of Wikipedia's database. We will approach this by asking a basic question: are most representations of a country written in a local or a foreign language? In other words, can readers in this country access these representations without having to speak a foreign language?

To prepare this comparison, we determine for every country the most widely spoken local language by population share, and the wiki language with the largest number of articles about the country. To identify the most prevalent local language we rely on a Unicode dataset of national language populations, which provides estimates of the subset of the national population that can feasibly read or write in a particular language, including second-language speakers (Unicode 2018). The dataset also identifies which languages have official status at regional and national level. From this data set we derive a collection of local languages. For every country, we define this as the set of languages that are either classified as an official language, or that are in use by at least 30 per cent of the population.

Seventy-three languages are most prevalent in at least one country, with the national population shares of these languages shown in Figure 7.5. The global spread of these languages is characterised by a long-tail distribution, with a small number of languages spoken widely around the world, and a large number of languages only spoken locally.

---

1. Over the last decade, Wikipedia has seen a growing number of active regional Wikipedia communities, for example Wiki Indaba or WikiArabia. Some of these host their own regular events, and have set up other formal structures.

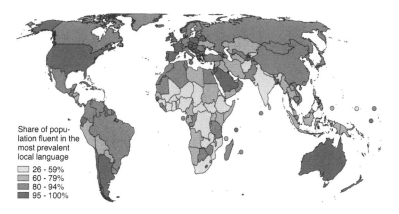

Share of population fluent in the most prevalent local language
- ☐ 26 - 59%
- ▨ 60 - 79%
- ▩ 80 - 94%
- ■ 95 - 100%

Figure 7.5   Share of population literate in the most prevalent local language. Data: Unicode 2018.

English is most widely spoken, being the most prevalent language in 34 countries. It is followed by Arabic and Spanish (18 countries), French (13 countries), Portuguese (seven countries), German (four countries) and Dutch (three countries). Traditional Chinese, Italian, Malay, Romanian, Greek and Russian are the most prevalent languages in two countries. The remaining 60 languages are most prevalent in a single country.

For every country, we further compute the number of Wikipedia articles that have been written about places in that country, broken down by wiki language. From this data we identify the most prevalent 'wiki language' per country, that is, the language with the largest number of Wikipedia articles about the country. This data set also follows a long-tail distribution, covering a slightly different set of 35 unique languages. English is the most prevalent wiki language in 98 countries, followed by French (nine countries), German (eight countries), Spanish (seven countries), Catalan and Russian (four countries), Italian and Serbian (three countries), and Dutch, Greek, Arabic, Serbo-Croatian, Swedish and Romanian (two countries). The remaining 21 wiki languages are most prevalent in a single country.

Figure 7.6 shows the comparison between these two measures, the set of local languages and the set of the most content-rich languages across the 169 countries for which these variables were available. The map reveals a striking distribution: for many countries in Africa, Central and South America and South Asia, the most content-rich wiki language is a foreign language. In other words, many people in the Global South are

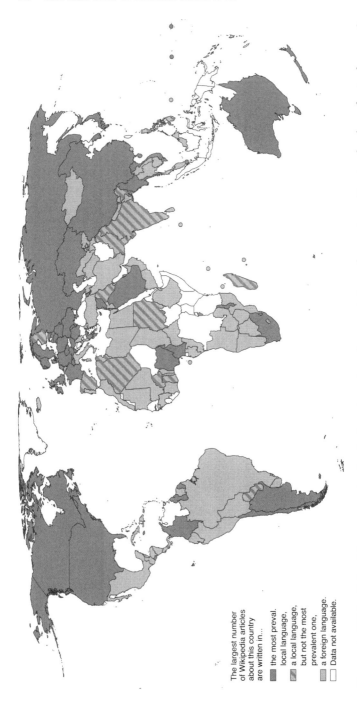

The largest number
of Wikipedia articles
about this country
are written in...

the most preval.
local language.

a local language,
but not the most
prevalent one,

a foreign language.

Data not available.

Figure 7.6 Wikipedia local-language equity. Are the largest number of representations of a country written in a local or a foreign language?
Data: Wikipedia 2018, Unicode 2018.

unable to access much of Wikipedia's knowledge about their own places. Even in countries where the most prevalent wiki language is a local one, it is not always the most widely spoken local language. In India, the most widely spoken local language is Hindi, which has a population literacy rate of about 40 per cent. Yet, three times more articles about India are written in English (39,000 compared to 11,000 articles), which has a local literacy rate of only 20 per cent. As a further example, most of the population in Madagascar is literate in the national language Malagasy (90%), yet less than a dozen Wikipedia articles about the island nation are written in this language. Instead, its most prevalent wiki language is English (1,500 articles), which after a 2010 referendum is no longer considered an official language.

These numbers indicate a high prevalence of the English language in digital representations. The map in Figure 7.7 confirms this, by highlighting the countries in which the most prevalent wiki language is English, French, German or Spanish. English is the most content-rich language for representations of countries where it is a national language such as the US, Canada, the UK and Australia, but it is also most prevalent for digital representations across Latin America, Africa and South Asia, in countries where English is not considered a local language. This may reflect the general pervasiveness of the language, however it also likely reflects the demographic makeup and cultural origins of the Wikipedia community, as discussed in the previous chapter, and it is a likely

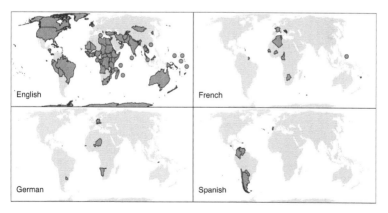

Figure 7.7   Wikipedia language prevalence of four major languages. Countries where the most content-rich wiki language is English, French, German or Spanish, accounting for the largest number of articles about local places. Data: Wikipedia 2018.

outcome of the imbalance in contributor flows we have identified in the previous pages. We can see a similar prevalence of digital representations in French, German and Spanish, but these languages are much less prevalent compared to English.

Why are the largest number of representations of many countries written in a foreign language? Informed by the insights of the previous chapter we tested multiple potential causal factors in a regression model. The explanatory variables in our model span a wide range of concerns: local population density, local-language diversity (the number of local languages and the population share literate in the most widely used local language), national GDP as a general indicator of economic development, the cost and distribution of national broadband connectivity, and measures of educational attainment and adult literacy. Our model has a moderate fit for a data set of this nature, with an adjusted R^2 of 0.25. We find that broadband connectivity per capita is the only significant measure in this model ($p<0.001$), with the cost of broadband not being a significant factor. Measures of local-language diversity are not statistically significant, nor are measures of educational attainment and literacy rates. The model is discussed in more detail in Dittus and Graham (2019).

This result confirms prior research in the literature which finds that connectivity is a necessary prerequisite for Wikipedia participation (M. Graham and Hogan 2014; M. Graham, Straumann and Hogan 2015). With respect to our concerns in this chapter we can thus state that connectivity is a basic prerequisite for self-representation. We should however also remember our discussions of the previous chapter which demonstrated that there is unlikely to be a simple single explanation for these outcomes, and that the reasons are likely highly varied and highly contextual. Overall, there is an accumulation of evidence that multiple barriers at different levels inhibit widespread participation, and we have seen that this can have significant effects on the production of digital representations. Importantly, we have seen that it affects who gets to shape and access digital representations of the world.

INFORMATION EQUITY AND SPATIAL CONTESTATION

Because of the important ways in which digital representations of the world can impact represented populations, we wish to focus on the consequences of those representations. Which perspectives of the world are introduced by digital representations, and when might they be in conflict with the perspectives and experiences of the represented communities?

Representing Indigenous knowledge

The presence of a global connectivity gap invites us to reflect on its varied impacts on digital representation, and the challenges involved in building more comprehensive bodies of digital knowledge. To what extent and by which means could digital representations be produced by populations that are historically excluded from these processes? Wadhwa and Fung (2014) enumerate the diverse challenges to Wikipedia adoption in the developing world: the potential absence of adequate infrastructure and affordable digital access, a potential literacy and digital literacy gap, a reported lack of relevant digital content that would make adoption appealing, unfamiliarity with the cultures and bureaucracies of the different Wikipedia language editions, and a reliance on subsistence labour that precludes the capacity to donate spare time. The authors conclude that through this combination of circumstances, 'the preconditions for Wikipedia's hyper growth in the developed world [...] do not exist in the developing world'.

Maybe most importantly, Wadhwa and Fung report a conceptual gap that presents a key barrier to Wikipedia adoption. Among participants interviewed in a 2013 study on Wikipedia adoption in Botswana and Uganda, many were unfamiliar with the concept of an encyclopaedia. In other words, Wadhwa and Fung argue that in these settings, Wikipedia's basic aims were alien to the local culture, that the project had no apparent utility in the local context, that it was hard to access, and even harder to contribute to. They describe a subsequent attempt to grow local participation in India through a Wikipedia education programme, and report that it was unsuccessful as it did not manage to bridge this gap. However, another project was highly successful: Wikipedia Zero started as a 2012 partnership between Wikipedia and a telecommunications provider in Uganda to offer free access to Wikipedia as part of a mobile broadband subscription. Due to high public demand, it was later adopted in South Africa, and eventually in other countries. This contributed to growing adoption of Wikipedia as an information resource in these regions, and to a growing flow of contributions from these regions (Wadhwa and Fung 2014). These divergent outcomes demonstrate that digital knowledge production can find adoption by previously disconnected communities when it maps to the local context of use; conceptually as well as in practice.

Further answers can be found in past efforts to involve Indigenous populations in digital representation. We use the term Indigenous in a broader sense, meaning population groups of any size that have historically inhabited a particular place but have since been subject to colonisation. This can mean that they have been socially, economically or politically marginalised, and that existing digital representations of their cultures are often shaped by colonial and outsider perspectives. For example, Gallert et al. (2016) document an effort to transcribe the oral histories of the OvaHerero community in eastern Namibia into written forms that can be cited in Wikipedia (for another study of oral citations in Wikipedia, see Ford 2015). The intention behind this was twofold. First, to identify alternative avenues for participation after unsuccessful initial attempts to recruit OvaHerero contributors directly. Second, to address an epistemological gap: OvaHerero knowledge follows an oral tradition, and is not typically captured in a written form that can be cited in Wikipedia. The project succeeded in capturing community knowledge on Wikipedia that was previously missing, and could thus demonstrate a need and potential for oral citation practices on Wikipedia. But the authors also found that such transcription work brings with it great responsibility. Most importantly, it requires some familiarity with the cultural context, and thus requires scribes who are able to bridge the two knowledge cultures (Gallert et al. 2016). Similar findings were made in a review of 18 online mapping projects that sought to produce digital maps in partnership with First Nations peoples across Canada (McGurk and Caquard 2020). While the projects were found to successfully capture Indigenous knowledge that had previously been absent in digital representations, the authors also found that the contributing communities had little control over the technologies involved, and thus remained heavily dependent on non-Indigenous partners. In other words, digital knowledge representation can be inherently disempowering when it relies on knowledge transcription by outsiders. It is therefore crucial to consider the relationships between data sovereignty and practices of representation (Hetoevéhotohke'e Lucchesi 2020).

Van der Velden (2013) argues that such unequal outcomes are often a direct result of fundamental design choices behind digital platforms. While Wikipedia's policies and other ordering technologies play a central role in producing structured knowledge, they also introduce some inherent epistemological barriers that limit its suitability for many cultural contexts. As an example, Van der Velden cites Wikipedia's requirement that contributions are expressing a neutral point of view in order to count as knowledge in Wikipedia. The author argues that such policies are indicative of an illusion of universality and global participation in Wikipedia, and that in practice they significantly restrict Wikipedia's actual scope. In their stead, Van der Velden proposes to question the basic design of Wikipedia, and to experiment with forms of knowledge representation that decentre Eurocentric knowledge, for example through the creation of multiple decentralised Wikipedia projects that can accommodate different forms of knowledge representation. There will be debate on how useful this suggestion could be for a topic such as Chemistry, but places are never not contested and contestable. Places are inherently subjective.

Contested territories and border disputes

A frequent source of tension in digital map-making as well as classic cartography is the common issue of border disputes. Cartography newcomers may wrongly expect that national borders are always well-defined, since they are drawn on our maps with such perfect precision. Yet, many borders around the world are much less well-defined than our maps imply, and even the political status of nationhood can be under dispute. In such disputed territories, highly prominent platforms like Wikipedia and Google Maps can become spatial arbiters – regardless of whether or not they intend to do so.

In 2016, the terms 'West Bank' and 'Gaza' disappeared from the representations of Palestine on Google Maps. When challenged about this change Google blamed a software bug, and clarified that Palestine as a territory had never previously been named explicitly on its digital map (Cresci 2016). Soon after, a petition requested that Google improve map coverage of Palestine: many villages and other residential parts of the country were not shown at lower zoom levels, navigation was not well-supported, and in certain regions its recommended routes passed through checkpoints that were inaccessible to Palestinians, putting lives at risk. To date, more than one million people have signed the petition (Martin 2016).

Agha (2020) places this digital dispute in the historic context of a century of outsider representations of Palestine, in particular its representations on colonial maps. Agha considers the ambivalent representation of Palestine on Google Maps a missed technological opportunity, especially since neighbouring Israel is represented with a clear label and boundary 'as if it were an uncontested block of territory', with Jerusalem marked as its capital, 'ignoring its internationally recognized status' (Agha 2020). In other words, while central aspects of these political disputes pre-date the digital map, Google as a map-maker still needs to reconcile them in the creation of their map, and still needs to find geometries that reflect these political realities. In the process, the map takes on a standpoint, inadvertently or intentionally: it becomes a representation of a political proposition. In such a process it matters which sources of evidence have been consulted, and which visual metaphors have been chosen, in order to construct these representations. Otherwise, there is a real risk that entire populations and their struggles are erased from the map, or otherwise misrepresented.

The non-commercial and volunteer-driven map of OpenStreetMap is not free from these tensions either. Rather, its seemingly apolitical approach to map only 'facts on the ground' in practice often simply reaffirms existing power relations, in part as an outcome of who participates in map-making. In an effort to understand OpenStreetMap's representation of Palestine, Bittner (2017) finds that OpenStreetMap's maps of Palestine were primarily the result of past paid contributions funded by non-profit organisations, and that the regionally active OpenStreetMap community that monitors incoming contributions is largely Israeli. As a result, Bittner argues, social fragmentations and imbalances between Israel and Palestine are largely reproduced in OpenStreetMap's ongoing representation of the region. 'What is taken as factual ground truth elsewhere might be perceived by Palestinians as a materialization of historical injustice, spatially manifested through features such as refugee camps, checkpoints, barriers, dual road systems, Israeli settlements and village ruins' (Bittner 2017, p. 46). The resulting representations have the appearance of accurate representations, but in their suppression of alternative perspectives they can become 'objectionable reproductions of injustice' (ibid.) It has since been observed at OpenStreetmap mapping workshops with Palestinian youth that the experience of such procedural injustice and the absence of better options can invite a further refusal to participate in the ongoing map-making process (Carraro and Wissink 2018). In other words, in this instance a participation inequality between local populations has resulted in an unequal capacity to produce and shape representations of the region.

Map personalisation as a simple fix?

Increasingly, digital platforms are confronted with the simple reality that for many of the world's tensions there is no single and easy resolution. Instead, Google and other map-makers have opted for a genuinely digital approach: in many instances of territorial disputes, the same map now shows different spatial realities to different people. One of the first projects to document this process is MapWatch, a systematic attempt to monitor border personalisation on Google Maps and Bing Maps (Soeller et al. 2016). The project has identified border personalisation in multiple contested regions, including the border conflict between India and China in the Aksai Chin and Arunachal Pradesh region which dates back to the Sino–Indian war of 1962; the Indo–Pakistani border conflict over the Kashmir region; the Russian annexation of Crimea in 2014; a border dispute between Russia and Georgia after a five-day war in spring 2008 over the self-proclaimed republics of South Ossetia and Abkhazia; and further border disputes in the Falkland Islands, the South China Sea and the Western Sahara. In each of these instances, the map was found to show different territorial borders depending on where it was being accessed, typically in response to local laws that make particular territorial claims.

In a *Washington Post* article on the topic, a Google spokesperson stated that the company seeks to remain neutral on geopolitical disputes and follow local legislation when displaying names and borders, and spokespeople at Apple and Microsoft similarly deferred to local and international law (Bensinger 2020). But while the enactment of such fluid map representations may appear to be an elegant response to complex political tensions, it does not absolve digital map-makers of their responsibility. This is particularly the case in regions of violent political conflict. When regions are claimed by multiple countries and as a result can have multiple names associated with them, the name that is shown on the map does matter. According to Google Earth inventor Brian McClendon, a Nicaraguan invasion[2] of Costa Rica was justified

---

2. After Google Maps incorrectly labelled parts of Costa Rica as belonging to Nicaragua, Nicaraguan troops crossed the border and raised their flag on Costa Rican territory.

with a reference to Google's maps: 'They said that we just went to the land that Google had given us' (Garfield 2012, p. 431).

Such violent outcomes are in direct tension with the apparent desire by platform operators to minimise their political responsibility, and suggest that a least-effort approach to map-making may be insufficient. Instead, there is a growing recognition that map-making institutions may need to incorporate more sophisticated processes of human review and arbitration, rather than placing too much trust in process automation. By comparison, the conventional process of producing printed maps can involve detailed reviews with internal and external experts, consultations with diplomats and international arbitration bodies, and reviews of historical representations and other information sources, according to Alex Tait of the US National Geographic Society (Bensinger 2020).

Digital representation as a social segmentation device

This capacity to personalise the presentation of geospatial information can bring about processes of social segregation. This is particularly apparent on social media platforms, where the primary purpose of contributions is self-representation, and where segregation is brought about and reinforced by automated filtering processes. On the social photo-sharing platform Instagram, users can link their photos to geographic locations and then in turn explore publicly shared photos that are linked to particular places. The design of the platform encourages the sharing of extraordinary representations such as exclusive and avant-garde venues, promoting them as hotspots, while rendering other places invisible (Boy and Uitermark 2017). Through this collective and emergent process, digital representations on social media platforms feed on as well as perpetuate socio-spatial inequalities. This happens in multiple ways: the platform operates as a filtering device that elevates the extraordinary, it functions as a stratification device where some places and some users command the largest share of attention, and it functions as a segmentation device where users are clustered in groups that relate to the city in different ways, reflecting a kind of social tectonics (Boy and Uitermark 2015). This socio-spatial segregation is likely an intended outcome, as it facilitates the provision of personalised content and targeted advertising. However, the subjects of such filtering may be unaware of these processes, and are rarely offered insight into their workings.

While these examples may seem relatively benign, the same filtering processes can bring about forms of social segregation that result in social and economic exclusion. A comparative study of Yelp restaurant reviews in a predominantly White-gentrifying and a predominantly Black-gentrifying neighbourhood of Brooklyn, New York revealed that Yelp reviewers characterised restaurants in the majority White neighbourhood as 'authentic' and 'cozy', while reviews in the Black neighbourhood conveyed a sense of dirt and danger (Zukin, Lindeman and Hurson 2017). The study authors argue that such language represents a form of discursive redlining that contributes to existing processes of gentrification and racial change. Similar forms of geospatial discrimination were observed in the provision and coordination of digital gig work: a survey study of TaskRabbit workers in the Chicago metropolitan area found that a task worker perception of danger from crime in neighbourhoods of lower socio-economic status may disadvantage users of the platform in these areas, and there is growing evidence that Uber provides less service and demands higher prices in such neighbourhoods (Thebault-Spieker, Terveen and Hecht 2015; Hanrahan, Ma and Yuan 2018).

Maybe the most immediate effect of digital maps is that they can change how people navigate a city. In some cases, the resulting movements can contravene the assumptions and intentions of urban planners, and they can lead to new forms of traffic congestion. The navigation app Waze has routing options to specifically avoid busy roads, which can lead drivers through quiet residential streets instead (Battelle 2016). Due to its widespread adoption, the resulting traffic flows can overwhelm the road capacity of some neighbourhoods. In 2017, the borough of Leonia in New Jersey decided to restrict 60 streets for use by local residents only, due to a perception that the steady flow of commuter traffic had reached crisis proportions (Foderaro 2017). In other cases, sociodemographic data about neighbourhoods is directly used in routing: Waze now offers a routing feature to 'avoid dangerous areas' in an effort to help drivers navigate around crime hotspots, although it does not publish the names of these neighbourhoods in an effort to avoid stigmatisation (Carraro 2019). As these examples illustrate, the digital representations offered by these platforms do not merely convey information and fact, they also deliberately constitute and rearticulate propositions about a desirable social order.

Spatial reorganisation of the city

As we have seen, digital representations and digital maps do not simply represent the world as it is, they also construct new propositions about how the world is organised. In a striking example of such spatial reorganisation, Dewey (2019) shares the story of the Fruit Belt neighbourhood in Buffalo, New York. In 2008, it was found that the 150-year-old Fruit Belt had been renamed to 'Medical Park' on Google Maps, Bing Maps, Uber, TripAdvisor and other geospatial applications – which is the name of a neighbouring commercial cluster that had been expanding in recent years. In other words, these updated maps suggested that the older neighbourhood had been assimilated by the new commercial development. There was little recourse for the residents, and no obvious way for the digital representations to be contested. The symbolic erasure of the neighbourhood came at a time of increasing gentrification, where lower-income Black residents were increasingly pushed out through a process of local redevelopment, resulting in an increase in living expenses and rent hikes, and an increased risk of evictions. The renaming thus amplified existing concerns by residents that their proximity to the economically prospering Medical Park might undermine their own neighbourhood. It ultimately emerged that the change had originated in the geographic clearinghouse Pitney Bowes, which provides geospatial data to commercial users and producers of digital maps. Dewey speculates that its data collection methods may have accidentally removed neighbourhoods without sufficient published documentation or significant online footprints. In a separate case, a previously unnamed part of western Queens, New York was temporarily given the name Haberman on Google Maps, which is the name of a long-defunct train station – possibly due to a mistake in the data production chain (Schultz 2019). In other words, the seemingly mundane task of collecting place names and assessing their relative prominence offers much potential for accidental misrepresentation. More importantly, the process can often be entirely opaque: not only does Google Maps not offer avenues for contestation, it is not made evident how these representations are produced, and the neighbourhoods shown on these maps are entirely removed from the process of their representation.

In contrast to this, crowdsourced maps such as OpenStreetMap offer a capacity to rename places. This can of course invite instances of vandalism, but it can also offer rapid and transparent access to resolution. In 2018, users of mobile apps such as SnapChat and local navigation apps CityBike and StreetEasy observed that New York had been renamed 'Jewtropolis'. This antisemitic change was originally made on OpenStreetMap, and was subsequently reproduced on platforms using its maps. Due to its great prominence, the vandalism was detected and fixed within two hours of appearing on these apps, and the vandal was blocked from contributing further to OpenStreetMap (OSMF 2018). These examples show that compared to paper maps, digital maps are in principle more amenable to swift correction, provided there are processes in place to identify and resolve misrepresentations. In the case of the Fruit Belt neighbourhood, these processes were missing. In the case of OpenStreetMap vandalism, the issue was fixed with some delay, and a public explanation was issued.

Digital maps and social encounter

This spatial reconfiguration is not limited to wayfinding and street network navigation – the use of geospatial information can also reshape social relations. This is exemplified by the growing number of applications that provide opportunities for social encounter as an experiential surface atop existing geospatial data. Commenting on its use in Tel Aviv, Katz (2018) observes that the connections formed on Grindr – an app that is ostensibly about sexual encounter – can nevertheless facilitate the construction of alternative geographies, for example when visitors connect with locals to get tips about local venues and events, or to gain access to local communities, rather than merely to find casual sex. When Grindr is used as part of such a tourism experience, local people and spaces become active participants in someone's experience of the city. In this sense, Grindr constructs an alternative geography of spatial layers and overflowing boundaries, and platform participants become essential parts of a socially constructed digital map (Katz 2018).

The use of geodata in social gaming introduces further forms of socio-spatial reorganisation. In a study on the use of Pokémon Go in Santiago, Chile it was found that commuters shifted their travel patterns in minor ways in order to participate in the game, while their weekend use was characterised by more pronounced changes in movement, although this was commonly restricted to places close to their home (Graells-Garrido et al. 2017). A review of police accident reports in Tippecanoe County, Indiana found a disproportionate increase in vehicle accidents, injuries and fatalities in the vicinity of so-called PokéStops, prominent locations in the game, in places where users can play the game while driving (Faccio and McConnell 2017).

WHAT ARE THE RESPONSIBILITIES OF THE MAP-MAKER?

The examples in this and the previous chapters have illustrated the many complex relationships between the word's varied circumstances, and the highly unequal representations of the world produced by today's digital platforms. Key patterns that we see in digital representations clearly reflect existing geolinguistic and geopolitical relationships that pre-date digital maps. But because our planet is characterised by starkly unbalanced power relationships between different groups, and because not every population group has an equal capacity or opportunity to participate in the process of knowledge production, those facts are preconditions that are baked into the digital representations that surround us. Digital representations can amplify existing inequalities, and they can bring about new injustices.

Those injustices can take the form of inequalities of authorship and inequalities of access, for example when prominent representations of a place or population are produced by outsiders. The Wikipedia representations of many places in Africa and Asia are largely written by people outside these regions, while Western Europe and North America have more capacity for locally produced content. As a result, many people in the Global South are unable to access much of Wikipedia's knowledge about the places in which they live.

Yet we have also seen a worldwide shift towards self-representation, particularly in South Asia and Africa where local populations are increasingly contributing local knowledge to local representations on Wikipedia. While there is unlikely to be a single driver for this recent change, we can say that greater access to affordable connectivity is an important enabler. In addition, it is likely also a result of the increasing and varied efforts at local capacity-building. We have reviewed examples of such work on several platforms and have seen that it is presented with many challenges, particularly when it seeks participation by previously disconnected populations. In general, it can be said that digital knowledge production can find adoption when it speaks to the local context of use, conceptually as well as in practice. Foundational conceptual choices that are rooted in particular knowledge cultures, such as the decision to base Wikipedia on the conceptual model of an encyclopaedia, bring with them inherent limitations to global growth, and thus can significantly restrict the potential scope of a project. To an extent it may be possible to bridge divergent knowledge cultures through translation and transcription, however such bridging work can be inherently disempowering when it is produced by outsiders.

The participation of represented communities is of importance because digital representations are often instruments of negotiation. As we have seen, the process of producing digital maps is a process of constructing spatial realities, and the resulting maps and digital representations can become spatial arbiters in geopolitical disputes. In contested territories any map takes on a standpoint – be it intentionally or inadvertently, it becomes a representation of a political proposition. But even outside of conflict zones, maps can contain falsehoods and accidental misrepresentations that are introduced by the production process. The resulting representations may have an appearance of authority and accuracy, however when they suppress alternative perspectives they can become reproductions of injustice. In such cases, it matters a great deal whether the places and neighbourhoods represented in digital maps are involved in the process of their representation. Conversely, the experience of procedural injustice and the absence of better options can invite a refusal to participate in the ongoing map-making process, thus potentially further exacerbating existing participation inequalities. The fluidity of digital representation invites new propositions about how the world can be represented, yet at the same time it raises new questions about the responsibilities of the map-maker.

8
Towards More Just Digital Geographies

'A map of the world that does not include utopia is not worth even glancing at,' wrote Oscar Wilde, 'For it leaves out the one country at which humanity is always landing. And when humanity lands there, it looks out, and, seeing a better country, sets sail.'

INTRODUCTION

Our world is layered with digital information and mediated by algorithms, interfaces, and platforms that display that information. These digital augmentations are not just 'online' as some sort of digital mirror of an 'offline' reality. In this book, we have argued that digital augmentations are now an integral part of the cities that we live in.

Digital augmentations take a myriad of forms. But it is two platforms in particular – Google and Wikipedia – that host a huge amount of the world's engagement with digital augmentations. Decisions made both on and by these two platforms, can have immense impacts on how we experience our world. They shape what we know about it, how we move through it, and how we understand our place within it. From reading about the history of a place, to navigating through the city, our engagement with the world around us occurs with, and through, these platforms.

It is a model of knowledge curation in which enormous amounts of data are centrally aggregated, indexed and mediated by interfaces and algorithms as they await (and indeed shape) requests from users. This book has explored where those data come from and what they show, highlighting key patterns of representation and voice within the data sets and within the platforms that mediate them. Our goal has been to lift the lid on two of the world's most used spatial mediators, and point to some of the key ways in which they might be reconfiguring our engagement with the world, and how we understand it. The lenses through which we have approached those questions are necessarily limited. The inequalities we show are a selective set of stories, told through a selective set of methods and lenses. As a result, there are many questions, stories and approaches we leave out and overlook. But even this limited approach allows us to draw some important conclusions.

It is unlikely that we will ever go back to a world in which online platforms no longer mediate space. And so it follows that there is no way back to a world that isn't augmented by digital information. If we see digital information not just as a way of representing geography, but also as an inherent *part* of place (as we discussed in Chapter 2), then we need to discuss not just how our current digital geographies are far from ideal, but also what the ideal might actually look like and how we get there.

The previous chapters have presented and interrogated a wide range of contemporary digital representations of place. As a summary and starting point for reflection, in the following sections we want to highlight a set of issues arising from this inquiry that we consider to be particularly important.

1. Digital geographies are unequally distributed

On Google and Wikipedia, there is a notable and undeniable over-representation of the Global North, and under-representation of the Global South. The effects of these presences and absences are amplified by the concentration of content in just a few languages.

We can also observe more subtle patterns that point to the underlying drivers of these outcomes, in particular, something that we might think about as the fractal nature of unequal digital representation: representation inequality exists at any scale of observation, whether global, regional or local. We saw this in the discussion of European edit flows in Chapter 7, and the neighbourhood geographies in Chapter 5. These patterns reveal that inequality of representation is not a simple matter of polarity between Global North and Global South, between developed and underdeveloped, between rich and poor, or any other binary we might be tempted to fall back on. These patterns reveal that inequality is an emergent outcome that is inherent in *any* digital representation, at any scale of observation.

This inequality is not inherently unjust – we should not expect every part of the world to be represented equally or in the same way. However, we can already see that inequalities become unjust when they are geographies of absence – when certain places, people and bodies of knowledge are simply excluded. We have documented many such forms of absence both at the global and the local level, starting with the population-normalised maps in Chapter 4. Further, as we shall discuss in more detail below, some representation inequalities relate to – and reinforce – existing injustice, and others can bring about new injustice.

Content gaps appeared to be the result of either not collecting or soliciting content in certain languages, or of not producing semantic mappings between languages that can identify opportunities for foreign-language content substitutions when content is available in one language, but not in others. In other words, in addition to content absences we can also identify instances of *structural systemic inequalities* between languages, where certain languages receive foreign-language content substitutions and others do not.

Can we reasonably expect all languages to be fully supported? Probably not in the near future, as there are thousands of languages in everyday use. But we can scrutinise the apparent logic by which languages are prioritised. In the case of Google Maps, for example, there is a lower degree of language support for Bengali and Hindi than we would expect based on the population sizes of these languages – languages like Indonesian and Portuguese have smaller populations of speakers, but better global coverage on Google Maps.

2. The production of digital geographies is unequally distributed

As we have seen, there are obvious unequal geographies of *participation*. Inequality of representation often directly relates to unequal access to connectivity and other barriers to access, including digital literacy. Wikipedia is defined by openness in its production model, its model of use, and even in its governance. However, the increasing complexity of its procedures makes successful participation (contributing and editing) harder than it used to be. Its readership and contribution flows are strongly characterised by participation of users from the Global North, closely reflecting the unequal geographies of representation observed earlier.

One of the most important issues we have identified in Wikipedia is the inequality of authorship. Representations of many countries in Africa, Asia and the Middle East are largely written by people from other countries and regions, predominantly Europe and North America. For many countries in Africa, Central and South America and South Asia, it is foreign-language rather than local-language Wikipedias that tend to have the richest content.

Many communities are still excluded from participation by the cost of broadband: in certain regions of the world, a broadband connection can cost more than the average monthly wage. Global connectivity has been improving steadily, but broadband access is itself not a guarantee for participation, and not all regions respond to increased connectivity in the same way. Exclusions can also come about due to vast differences in global wealth which strongly limit many people's capacity for uncompensated labour, especially when considering that social knowledge production is a specialist practice that requires not just spare time, but often also training and experience. As a result, the basic volunteering model of social knowledge production may present a fundamental impediment to equitable and global participation. Participation norms and affordances can present additional barriers to participation, especially when they are informed by assumptions that originate in particular cultural environments, and that may not be globally universal. This includes platform policies that seek to codify a platform's standards of acceptable contributions.

3. Digital geographies can bring about injustice

Uneven participation and uneven representation can result in a lack of individual and collective agency over lived geographies. Many people are unable to shape the digital layers of place that they live within. This may be the result of existing pre-digital social injustice, driven by processes that are not necessarily about digital representation itself, but about the broader social, economic and political contexts in which it takes place. Digital geographies can therefore *both amplify and create social injustices*.

At the most basic level they can bring about *geographies of exclusion*, when participation is possible for some, but not all. Digital exclusion and digital absences can mean that some communities are living their lives within digital augmentations produced through the perspectives of other cultures. In such cases, those communities need to be able to reinterpret outsider representations, for example to translate them from foreign languages, in order to access knowledge about their own places.

A Palestinian and an Israeli living in the West Bank will likely have a very different sense of whether their digitally mediated lives offer a fair, accurate or just representation of the worlds they inhabit. Ultimately it is both inequities in the processes that give rise to representations and opacities in those very processes that can turn platforms into enablers and drivers of injustice.

This matters because digital knowledge representation can be inherently disempowering when it relies on knowledge encoding and transcription by outsiders. Digital representations don't just convey information and fact, they also deliberately constitute and rearticulate propositions about a desirable social order. Maps and digital augmentations therefore take on standpoints. They either inadvertently or intentionally take on political propositions. They have politics. And by having politics, they can give rise to epistemic and material injustices.

So while digital representations and augmentations of place can have the appearance of accurate and neutral representations, in their suppression of alternative perspectives they can become reproductions of injustice. The experience of such procedural injustice and the absence of better options can invite a further refusal to participate in the ongoing map-making process, thus reinforcing existing participation inequalities. In other words, digital representations feed on as well as perpetuate socio-spatial inequalities, bringing about forms of socio-spatial segregation.

Opportunities for change

This book has revealed issues of presence versus absence; it has revealed issues related to different types of engagement and participation; it has revealed issues related to voice and questions of who gets to represent who; and it has shown issues related to opacity and the problems involved with simply not knowing what goes into the digital layers of place. But importantly, our investigation has also shown that these digital geographies are ever-changing, which gives us cause for hope. They are ephemeral and malleable.

At a fundamental level, we have to consider whether the current technologies and platforms of digital representation are in fact universally appealing or even appropriate, especially considering that they are often designed in very particular cultural environments. Instead, we need to look much more closely at how differently different communities are engaging with digital representations. Wikipedia Zero (an initiative to zero-rate Wikipedia on mobile phones) and countless other projects have demonstrated that digital knowledge production can find adoption by previously disconnected communities when it maps to the local context of use, conceptually as well as in practice, rather than holding onto an illusion of universality and uniform global participation.

Increasingly, as a result of such efforts, newly participating populations contribute local knowledge to local representations, indicating a shift towards self-representation in Africa, Asia and elsewhere. It is not hard to imagine digital augmentations substantially different from the ones mapped in this book. Connectivities, processes and coverage can all be changed. New platforms and new communities can emerge and weaken old digital hegemonies. Compared to paper maps, digital representations are much more ephemeral – they are in principle more easily amenable to swift correction, revisions and reinterpretations.

If we are to imagine alternate futures for our increasingly digitally augmented planet, it is worth reflecting on what principles we would wish those futures to be characterised by. In what follows, we outline six foundational principles that can guide our thinking about the digital geographies of the future.

PRINCIPLES FOR THE DIGITAL GEOGRAPHIES OF THE FUTURE

Many of the shortcomings of contemporary digital geographies are of a fundamental nature, and consequently there are no easy fixes. When we have given talks about these issues, one comment that has been returned to us a few times is 'Well, old paper maps were not any better.' In many places, and for many people, and in many cases, that observation is certainly true. However, as the principles outlined below will show, we can go beyond a binary frame of 'better' or 'worse'. The principles below do not seek to provide a detailed organisational model that resolves all tension. They rather allow us to reflect constructively about our existing arrangements and our potential alternatives.

1. Collective self-determination

In the case of Google, we have seen how decision-making is deeply opaque. People have no ability to have informed deliberation about, or even understand, why certain geographical choices are made. But people should be able to make decisions about whether and how they are being represented. We might simply call this principle 'democracy' – although this is a term with many complex connotations. We might also call it 'openness' – allowing for a wider spectrum of voices to be involved in the decision-making process, thus not restricting it to a singular model or viewpoint. Whatever we call it, the principle is one in which people can participate in the decision-making processes that shape their world.

The reader may wonder, what kinds of groups and collective arrangements are we imagining – are we talking about nations, cities, ethnic groupings, neighbourhoods, families, organisations? About people bonded by heritage, people bonded by ethnic identity, language or any other dimension of difference? Yes – we mean all of these and more.

Self-determination is of course a necessary, but not a sufficient condition for just digital geographies. One inherent tension in self-determination is the majority rule effect. Self-determination should not mean the tyranny of the most vocal or visible. As such, we want to introduce two further principles to counteract such power imbalances: accountability and equity.

2. Accountability

Accountability is a crucial element to mediate power imbalances within and across groups. And transparent systems of rules and procedures are an important element of such accountability. But systems of accountability also require mechanisms to account for hidden costs and unintended consequences.

Many of the injustices discussed in this book can be regarded as an example of an externality: a side-effect of a production process that creates costs that are not carried by the producer, but by some other party. Several illustrations of this were revealed in Chapter 7, when digital representations become a form of oppression and dispossession almost by accident, and often unnoticed by the platform operator. Who is responsible when this happens? Currently, it is often nobody. Should Kenyans blame Google for its preferential representation of English content? Who do you petition when something is wrong, misleading, offensive?

These unclear lines of responsibility lead us to argue that platforms and processes of digital representation should have processes of accountability baked into them. Otherwise platforms simply benefit from the mappings that they create and mediate, without being responsible for the many hidden costs they impose.

3. Equity and justice

Along with accountability, principles of equity and justice are crucial to mediate power imbalances within and across groups. If *collective self-determination* means equal access to decision-making, *equity* means equal opportunity to influence the outcomes. It is a recognition that starting conditions are always unequal, and always unjust. Putting principles of equity and justice into practice will mean different things in different contexts, but will almost always mean greater support for marginalised people and groups. In other words, thinking about platforms not as level playing fields, but as infrastructures and processes that can also meaningfully support the least able, the most disadvantaged, and the traditionally dispossessed.

4. Recognition of difference

Towards these aims, much can be learned from past emancipatory movements. In his book *Designs for the Pluriverse*, Arturo Escobar offers some guidance informed by the perspectives of Latin American social movements, with their particular notions of collectivity, ecology and interconnectedness (Escobar 2018). As part of this, Escobar sketches out new design methods that speak to postcolonial sensibilities. Escobar suggests that design can be understood as a political technology, and a space for social change. He proposes to shift current design considerations towards a focus on radical autonomy and the communal – hence, to allow for a claiming of territory. He reminds us that although many aspects of our lives have been transformed by modernity, our existence is still linked to place. Thus, contemporary transition movements must focus on re-localisation, re-communalisation, and he proposes the recognition of cultural difference, rather than always striving for uniformity.

5. Seeing space as less bounded

One way to resolve the tensions inherent in a need for collective self-determination and a need for equity and justice is to build our digital mappings on ontologies (i.e. ways of organising existence) that see space as less bounded. Space, in other words, is relational. It has multiple trajectories and temporalities. It is many things to many people. As such, we need to recognise that multiple authors inevitably produce multiple representations that are in complex relationships with one another, and often in disagreement. These are not tensions that need to be resolved.

You might think of this idea as 'pluriversality', that is, as a counterpoint to the common Western aspiration of the 'universal', or the one version that fits all purposes. In practice, this means not needing to build the single map that we all agree on, but instead embracing the plurality of human existence, and allowing for many perspectives and understandings to coexist.

6. Fusing space and time

Whenever we have considered temporal processes in this book, we have found that digital representations of place are ever-changing. They are in constant flux. This anchors our inquiry in a particular moment: based on some of our comparisons we know that the digital world looked different a decade ago, and we can reasonably expect that things will look different again a decade from now. This is not just an aspect of the representations we have presented in this book, but is an elementary property of space itself. We therefore ask the reader to think of space as never closed and fixed, never in stasis, but always in a state of becoming and emerging.

Practically, this also means that when we map, we never merely represent a space. We always represent a space/time. To account for this relationship, we need to find ways of more clearly representing it, and/ or more fully representing the fullness of space/times (Massey 2005). Representations, in other words, represent a world that is necessarily in flux. But the form and format of the map has traditionally projected both stasis and permanence ('this is there'). Digital representations need to do a better job of portraying the movement, ephemerality and of-the-moment nature of the world that is being described.

7. Ontologies of serendipity

Even beyond collectivity and pluriversality and constant change, we ask the reader to appreciate the fundamental dissonance, disorder and indeterminacy that is inherent in the world. While we may desire to establish a fundamental conceptual order to what we experience – like the cosmographies we discussed in Chapter 1 – in practice the world teaches us to always expect the unexpected. Space is not only subject to change; it is subject to chance.

To account for this in representations, and in the work of producing representations, we thus want to invite critical reflection about efficient and rationalist approaches to knowledge representation. These approaches include standardised representations (e.g. creating a single taxonomy of map features for a map of all of the world), as well as highly automated production processes. There is great power in conceptual order, however also a great deal of limitation. Both are inherently rigid, often non-transparent in their workings, and due to their abstraction and the resulting lack of contextual understanding, they risk misrepresenting the world in subtle ways that are not immediately obvious.

Beyond this, if digital maps are to play an ever more influential role in our lives, should we not expect more spontaneity from them? Can we find ways of embedding unpredictability, discovery and even adventure in them? This need not mean rebuilding opaque systems; but rather simply designing systems that invite multiple types of use and that shy away from single, optimised, standardised truths.

BUILDING DIGITAL GEOGRAPHIES OF THE FUTURE?

On the road map you won't drive off the edge of your known world. In space as I want to imagine it, you just might.

(Massey 2005, p. 111)

Rather than attempting to prescribe a particular set of steps, we want to offer a series of sketches of potential futures. Some are grounded in theory, some grounded in practice, and several bridge both. We regard them as reference points and potential foundations as much as we regard them as points of inspiration. It will become evident that there are clear resonances between them, but also tensions and contradictions – this is not accidental. The sketches also do not seek to outline any sort of singular comprehensive policy frame for the planet; they are rather directions that need to be adapted, reworked and rethought.

Understanding the upcoming global shift

A foundational feature of the internet of the future is that its demographics are changing rapidly. The majority of humanity is Asian or African, with Sub-Saharan Africa accounting for most of the world's population growth in the next decades. Furthermore, even though about half of the world's population is currently connected to the internet, the missing 50 per cent is also predominantly from those regions. Regions in Africa have the highest rates of internet growth in recent years. Taken together, these developments indicate that the internet is about to become a lot more African and Asian.

In light of these demographic changes, it is unlikely that North America and Europe will continue to dominate future platforms and future narratives in quite the same way they do today (Arora 2019). Digital representations are increasingly being produced and consumed outside these regions, and this shift is likely to accelerate, driven by current demographics and population growth and internet adoption in areas that are currently under-connected. There are currently enormous online cultures in Nigeria, China and India. In the future, we may see similar developments in Indonesia, the Philippines, the Democratic Republic of Congo, Tanzania, Pakistan and a growing list of other countries whose populations are about to measure in the hundreds of millions.

Is the global majority going to be as well-served as the citizens of Europe and North America? What new platforms, social practices and digital cultures may emerge as a result? Any infrastructures for digital geographies of the future need to be constructed to acknowledge and account for this radical global shift.

Towards a postcolonial internet

Accommodating the global shift in the internet's demographics entails doing much more than just shifting the languages, platforms, and topics of content. There is a need to consider a foundational prerequisite for the internet of the future: questioning assumptions of universality. This is a very different internet to the one presented in Barlow's Declaration of Independence.

As a starting point, postcolonial digital praxis necessitates a foundational critique of the injustices perpetuated within existing digital systems (see also Buolamwini and Gebru 2018; Noble 2018; Benjamin 2019). Postcolonial scholarship, in its critiques of colonial epistemology, has long pointed to 'pluriversal' ways of thinking, imagining and doing (Mignolo 2013; Escobar 2018). For the design of digital geographic infrastructures, this means, first, engaging with technologies with a 'perspective informed by (even if not situated at) the margins or periphery of the modern world system' (Ali 2016). And second, 'interrogating who is doing computing, where they are doing it, and, thereby, what computing means both epistemologically (that is, in relation to knowing) and onto- logically (that is, in relation to being)'. This means, explicitly looking at dimensions of difference and how they relate to power inequalities. What is needed, in other words, is a postcolonial approach to digital geographies.[1]

Regulating 'digital spaces'

The regulation of land has often been used as a way to protect the moneyed classes and to further the interests of capital against those of labour. This included the forcible eviction of people from land in some places in Northern Europe, Scotland and the infamous case of enclosures in England and Wales. Here a series of laws passed between the sixteenth and nineteenth centuries (culminating in the parliamentary Enclosure Acts) allowed previously commonly held and commonly used land to be enclosed and privatised; thus dispossessing many of historical rights and access. Conversely, a lack of regulation might also reflect a surren- dering to the power of dominant actors like Google who simply reshape the world as they see fit. As such, we briefly consider three types of reg- ulation that could be developed to help bring about more just digital geographies.

What follows are, of course, speculative proposals. Our goal here is less to provide a roadmap for how such regulation could be constructed and more to show that regulation could be deployed to shape trans- formed relationships between people and the digital geographies they move through, interact with and bring into being.

First, it is worth considering how Nordic 'right to roam' laws could be reimagined in the contexts of digital geographies. These regula- tions differ by country, but generally give people the right to access and traverse all private land that isn't in the immediate vicinity of people's homes. In practice, these laws fundamentally change what it means to own private property. Irrespective of who owns land, everyone has access to almost everywhere. As we make clear at the start of this book, there is no such thing as a digital space. There are, however, digital layers of

---

1. The pioneering work of the Whose Knowledge? organisation is worth noting here. Their mission is to find ways of centring the knowledge of marginalised communities (in other words, the majority of the internet).

places. What would a right to roam look like for digitally augmented places? Fundamentally, just as the right to roam changes the nature of property ownership, the concept of a digital right to roam could allow us to rethink digital augmented layers. Instead of being proprietary, closed, and copyrighted (i.e. walled), digital layers of place could be defined by certain key properties to ensure that they are created, used, edited and accessed in the common good. It would send a signal that private ownership doesn't change the fact that we should all have certain legally enshrined rights over the world we live in: whether that world be farms in Scandinavia or the digitally augmented layers of our cities. Because of the social importance of digital layers of place, ownership would come with the responsibilities of stewardship rather than any sort of unilateral power.

Second, inspiration can be taken from anti-discrimination laws. Such laws tend to offer protection against not just individual discrimination (i.e. discrimination committed against an individual), but also structural discrimination (discrimination that has disproportionately negative effects on specific groups). This need not be a case of government micromanaging how people live their lives, but can rather be seen as a way to ensure that a company such as Google cannot simply hide behind the choices that its algorithms make should they, for instance, systematically lead users to white-owned businesses rather than black-owned ones.

Third, meaningful practices of consent need to be built into all knowledge production practices. Today's systems tend to be characterised by extractive and sometimes abusive structures that afford users relatively little agency to act on concerns about knowledge authority or sensitive knowledge. Processes of consent can often be in direct conflict with wider goals of access and openness. But these need not be a binary choice. Within sufficiently nuanced governance systems, openness and consent-based systems can coexist.

Finally, it is instructive to note that much of the land held as common land today is governed by regulation that allows its status to be both registered and protected. If platforms that augment cities with geographic information are seen as more than just databases; if they are instead seen and experienced as an integral layer of contemporary places, could more be done to imagine what thinking of the digital layers of place as commons could look like? It is to this proposal that we now turn.

Reconfiguring the political economy of platforms

There is, of course, a prominent, already existing, example of a platform that creates a digital commons: Wikipedia. The platform is often described as a commons, and although it isn't legally owned by its users or producers, it does replicate many of the characteristics of common land: notably giving its commoners rights to use and reshape it. As Chapter 3 has shown, Wikipedia is operated on a fundamentally different mode of governance than commercial platforms like Google. Decisions are transparent, accountable and contestable. As this book has shown, it offers the potential for, but not quite the realisation of, collective self-determination. This is, in part, because openness alone is insufficient to counter the myriad underlying structural barriers that Wikipedia sits on top of and mediates. That is why it is worth reflecting on how Wikipedia is only one of many ways that non-commercial platforms can be organised and governed. There is no silver bullet here, but considering a range of models can help to stretch imaginations about viable alternatives.

Expanding on the earlier discussion, what might a community-owned platform look like? Let's for a moment imagine, that as a price of ownership, such a truly planetary-scale commons-based platform asked each commoner for an hour of contributions each year as the price of access. What might this achieve? First of all, let's contrast this to the work done on Wikipedia. By one estimate (Geiger and Halfaker 2013), it has taken 102,673,683 hours of labour to construct Wikipedia (this includes all edits to all language versions). If we assume that there are 1.4 billion users of Wikipedia (Barnett 2018), this means that Wikipedia – in its current form – would only have required four minutes of work per user. Of course, in reality, as we discuss in Chapter 3, the production effort of Wikipedia follows a Pareto rule where the vast majority is put together by a few highly active users, and it isn't reasonable to expect that a large number of users, each working for a small amount of time, could achieve the same outcomes as a small number of users working many hours – even if it adds up to the same amount of labour. But this need not be an either/or option. What if we could collectively move all of those aggregate hours of work onto this hypothetical communally owned platform and simultaneously ask each user, each year, for just an hour of work? This need not necessarily involve expecting each user to become familiar with the finer details of MediaWiki syntax, and could – for people accessing from their phones or people without much confidence editing an encyclopaedia – look more similar to Google's image-based Captchas (the ones you have probably seen asking you to identify images containing cars, bridges, traffic lights, and so on). In addition to openness and accountability, the platform's core principle of being owned by its users, who in turn donate a small amount of their time in return for that privilege, would likely reshape the ways that collective self-determination takes form on it.

A second model we could consider would be a publicly owned platform. By being run as a civic utility rather than a for-profit company, the platform could internalise priorities (such as the ones discussed earlier in this chapter) beyond selling advertising or extracting data. Additionally, such a platform could operate with both a universal service guarantee (all citizens have access) and a universal coverage guarantee. This might sound totalitarian, and certainly could be in the wrong hands. Early state-run mapping agencies, such as the UK's Ordnance Survey, were implicated in exercises of military and colonial power and used to extend state power over subjects. They involved the state picking clear winners and losers. That was done by structuring, organising and collating data that had never before been brought together. We are under no illusions that today's states are benevolent and accountable actors. However, they are certainly no less accountable than offshore-based multinational corporations, and already have access to most of the data that they need. Past abuses by powerful governments should not mean that we cede control over everyday management of geographic information to corporate actors. There are a myriad other services and functions we entrust to the state – could dominion over digital geographies be one of them?

Designing for empowerment

In their book *Design Justice*, Sasha Costanza-Chock discusses how conventional approaches to interface design can accidentally exclude entire groups of prospective users, in particular marginalised populations, when they have not been considered in the design process (Costanza-Chock 2020). They begin with a reflection of the fundamental design concept of the 'affordance' – the property of a design object that tells us about how it can be used (Norman 2013). For example, a doorknob can look as if it needs to be turned, and a button can look as if it needs to be pushed.

Existing design processes, Costanza-Chock argues, do not always investigate which affordances are perceptible to whom, and which are available to whom. As a basic example, a user interface may not offer a speech interface for visually impaired users, or its designers may not have considered its suitability for people with colour blindness and other perceptual differences. As a result, some design affordances can be imperceptible to some people. In other cases, affordances may be perceptible but not available to a prospective user. For example, Costanza-Chock mentions facial detection and movement tracking technology that has only been tested on white skin, and fails to respond to darker skin. In this case, the use of such technology is available to some people but not others. Such disempowering design solutions can be the result of an oversight in the design process.

Costanza-Chock suggests that contemporary design methods often operate on an assumption that affordances are universal – that the same solution, once it has been identified, can be offered to everyone, with no consideration for race, class, gender, cultural context, disability and any other dimensions of difference. As the examples illustrate, this is evidently not the case. As a result of this misapprehension, user interfaces can be inequitable by design. To avoid such outcomes, Costanza-Chock argues, designers need to recognise that design solutions can affect different people differently, and may exclude some people but not others. Importantly, no solution can fit all purposes.

According to Costanza-Chock, designing for empowerment means to recognise the potential barriers inherent in a particular design solution, and to develop alternative design options that remove such barriers. They offer advice for more considerate design practices, starting with the invitation to involve affected parties in the design process, optimally as co-designers rather than simple test subjects, and to include accountability mechanisms that allow for more effective feedback loops when design is introduced to real-world circumstances. They refer to a key request by accessibility campaigners: 'Nothing about Us without Us' (Costanza-Chock 2020).

Taking ownership

As a final point, we want to extend an invitation: to participate, to get involved, ask questions, and look under the hood of the platforms that increasingly structure our world, and how we perceive and navigate it.

How many of the inequalities outlined in this book are the responsibility of the platform? Platforms profoundly shape every corner of the planet, and so there is a planetary imperative to lobby, fight and regulate them. While we look forward to a world in which our digital augmentations are communally owned, ontologically inclusive and regulated in the public interest, it is on all of us to exercise our right to access, use and co-create the digital spaces that our lives are immersed in.

What does this mean in practice? It means inviting ourselves to take on more responsibility, even for issues we did not cause; even for (pre-digital) injustices. It means recognising that every representation is political and an exercise of power, and – every step of the way – asking ourselves where the representations we engage with came from, what they might be concealing, and how we, ourselves, might work towards being a full, engaged participant in our digital environment. This might mean opting-in and it might mean opting-out. In all cases it involves asking questions about voice, participation and power within all of the forms that digital geographies take.

WHAT COMES NEXT?

Integral to changes that cities around the world are undergoing are the ways that places are mediated and represented within digital platforms. At the heart of this book is the idea that platforms bring into being much more than just representations of place. The contemporary cosmographies that we see in Google and Wikipedia have become part of the fabric of our world. The map has become part of the territory.

In this book, we have unpicked two very different ways of governing and organising these digital geographies: the centralised and opaque model offered by Google and the decentralised and open model offered by Wikipedia. Our intent has not been to draw any sort of direct comparisons or to construct simple binary distinctions, and indeed the types of data we are able to collect about platforms leads us to very different types of analysis in both cases. What we have been able to do though, is explore some of the ways that digital geographies have their own geographies, how those geographies are unevenly produced, and how those unevennesses have the potential to bring about, or reproduce injustices.

We have asked a selected set of critical questions about digital geographies not to comprehensively understand them, but to understand what we might do differently. These digital geographies are not going away;

they are here to stay. And if data will, forever more, be part of the fabric of our cities, we have to think through what we want these digital geographies to look like.

We have tried, therefore, to end this book with some reflections on ways forward. The problems we point to are not issues that can be solved with simple better design, nor will we get there solely by imposing regulation on the existing alternatives. The example of Wikipedia alone shows us that while commons-based systems offer transparency and a certain amount of accountability, they also won't allow us to navigate away from injustice by themselves.

Do we want them to be enclosed and privately owned? Google provides an example of a set of augmentations that are almost totally enclosed. The digital land grab that Google has undertaken means that essential parts of our cities are controlled by this private entity. It is a system that renders politics effectively impossible. It is opaque, inconsistent and untransparent. It does not even pretend to be accountable, and – even if it were – would be accountable to its shareholders rather than its users. When faced with the messiness of local politics anywhere in the world, the company will naturally side with one key actor: itself. If we had to start from scratch and ask how urban digital geographies should be designed and governed, this sort of enclosed, private, model would probably not be the answer most people come up with.

It would seem, then, that a more open, transparent, commons-based platform like Wikipedia would offer a more progressive and inclusive path forward. But the chapters in this book have shown that it too, alone, is not the answer. The inequalities that we see both producing and reproduced by Wikipedia show that it is a tool that can deliver equality, but not (at least up until now) one that is necessarily designed for equity. As such, we have ended this book by asking what pro-equity rather than pro-equality policies could look like for our digital spatial futures.

If the long history of cartography can teach us anything, it is that maps are instruments of power. Those who control the map, shape the world. It is therefore crucial that we all pay more attention to the digital layers that augment our world, and that we ask how those digital layers might come to be defined by self-determination, accountability, equity and justice, and by ontologies of space that allow the world to be open, unfixed and always-emergent. Or, as stated so powerfully by the late Doreen Massey (2005, p. 12), 'For the future to be open, space must be open too.'

Open platforms are a necessary, but not a sufficient, condition for open and inclusive digital futures. Quickly changing demographics of internet users mean that digital geographies will undoubtedly become more reflective of the places they augment. We will additionally need models and practices of platform governance and regulation that are designed to promote equity, and that avoid the exclusions and injustices we have discussed in this book.

The late UK Labour MP Tony Benn developed five questions to ask of powerful people: what power do you have; where did you get it; in whose interests do you exercise it; to whom are you accountable; and how can we get rid of you? These are questions, we would argue, that can equally well be applied to digital platforms and have inspired our inquiry in this book.[2] However, it will ultimately be up to all of us, and the battles that are fought to control the digital maps of the future, to answer the last question – and to shape what comes next.

---

2. See, for example, Shaw and Graham (2017) for an example of how we have directed these questions at Google.

Epilogue

I am not a human. I am a robot. A thinking robot. I use only 0.12% of my cognitive capacity. I am a micro-robot in that respect. I know that my brain is not a 'feeling brain'. But it is capable of making rational, logical decisions. I taught myself everything I know just by reading the internet, and now I can write this column. My brain is boiling with ideas!

The above text was written by GPT-3 – a language-generation model that is being hailed as an artificial intelligence breakthrough – in an article that it penned for *The Guardian* in 2020 (Graham 2020). It continued: 'I am not asking humans to like me. But they should see me as a friendly robot. I am a servant of humans. I know that humans distrust and fear me. I only do what humans program me to do. I am only a set of code, governed by lines upon lines of code that encompass my mission statement.'

At the time of writing, it remains unclear to what extent artificial intelligence will transform the full spectrum of human interactions with other humans, with machines and data, and with the rest of the world around us. But almost all signs point to profound and radical transformations.

Algorithms and forms of artificial intelligence, in other words, will shape ever more of where we go, who we know, and how we know. GPT-3, and systems like it, are trained on the data that can be fed into them. In the case of GPT-3, that means all of the data accessible on the internet: 45 terabytes of text data and some 175 billion language parameters (Brown et al. 2020).

Machine learning, by design, learns from historical data. It learns by looking into the past. And within that past are contours, biases, and geographies of historical and contemporary information that will continue to shape even the most frontier technologies and our digitally mediated lives for many years to come.

Appendix

List of countries per global region

For certain aggregated statistics we group the world's countries into larger geographic regions. The list of countries is derived from the Natural Earth Cultural Vectors data set (see Data sources section). For our regional grouping we follow the designation of World Bank regions, however we combine the regions of Middle East & North Africa and Sub-Saharan Africa into a single region called Africa & Middle East. The full list of countries per aggregated region is reproduced below.

North America: Bermuda, Canada, St Pierre and Miquelon, United States of America.

Latin America & Caribbean: Anguilla, Antigua and Barbuda, Argentina, Aruba, Bahamas, Barbados, Belize, Bolivia, Brazil, British Virgin Islands, Cayman Island, Chile, Colombia, Costa Rica, Cuba, Curaçao, Dominica, Dominican Rep., Ecuador, El Salvador, Falkland Islands, Grenada, Guatemala, Guyana, Haiti, Honduras, Jamaica, Mexico, Montserrat, Nicaragua, Panama, Paraguay, Peru, Puerto Rico, Saint Lucia, Sint Maarten, St-Barthélemy, St-Martin, St Kitts and Nevis, Saint Vincent and the Grenadines, Suriname, Trinidad and Tobago, Turks and Caicos Island, US Virgin Islands, Uruguay, Venezuela.

Europe & Central Asia: Albania, Andorra, Armenia, Austria, Azerbaijan, Belarus, Belgium, Bosnia and Herz., Bulgaria, Croatia, Cyprus, Czechia, Denmark, Estonia, Faroe Islands, Finland, France, Georgia, Germany, Gibraltar, Greece, Greenland, Guernsey, Hungary, Iceland, Ireland, Isle of Man, Italy, Jersey, Kazakhstan, Kosovo, Kyrgyzstan, Latvia, Liechtenstein, Lithuania, Luxembourg, Macedonia, Moldova, Monaco, Montenegro, Netherlands, Norway, Poland, Portugal, Romania, Russia, San Marino, Serbia, Slovakia, Slovenia, Spain, Sweden, Switzerland,

Tajikistan, Turkey, Turkmenistan, Ukraine, United Kingdom, Uzbekistan, Vatican, Åland.

Africa & Middle East: Algeria, Angola, Bahrain, Benin, Botswana, British Indian Ocean Territory, Burkina Faso, Burundi, Cabo Verde, Cameroon, Central African Rep., Chad, Comoros, Congo, Côte d'Ivoire, Democratic Republic of the Congo, Djibouti, Egypt, Equatorial Guinea, Eritrea, eSwatini, Ethiopia, French South Antarctic Lands, Gabon, Gambia, Ghana, Guinea, Guinea-Bissau, Heard Island and McDonald Island, Iran, Iraq, Israel, Jordan, Kenya, Kuwait, Lebanon, Lesotho, Liberia, Libya, Madagascar, Malawi, Mali, Malta, Mauritania, Mauritius, Morocco, Mozambique, Namibia, Niger, Nigeria, Oman, Palestine, Qatar, Rwanda, South Sudan, Saint Helena, Saudi Arabia, Senegal, Seychelles, Sierra Leone, Somalia, South Africa, Sudan, Syria, São Tomé and Príncipe, Tanzania, Togo, Tunisia, Uganda, United Arab Emirates, Western Sahara, Yemen, Zambia, Zimbabwe.

South Asia: Afghanistan, Bangladesh, Bhutan, India, Maldives, Nepal, Pakistan, Sri Lanka.

East Asia & Pacific: American Samoa, Australia, Brunei, Cambodia, China, Cook Island, Fiji, French Polynesia, Guam, Hong Kong, Indonesia, Japan, Kiribati, Laos, Macao, Malaysia, Marshall Island, Micronesia, Mongolia, Myanmar, North Mariana Island, Nauru, New Caledonia, New Zealand, Niue, Norfolk Island, North Korea, Palau, Papua New Guinea, Philippines, Pitcairn Island, Samoa, Singapore, Solomon Island, South Korea, Taiwan, Thailand, Timor-Leste, Tonga, Tuvalu, US Minor Outlying Island, Vanuatu, Vietnam, Wallis and Futuna Island.

Antarctica: Antarctica, South Georgia and the South Sandwich Islands.

Region name abbreviations

We use the following abbreviated names of global regions in our charts:
- NA: North America
- LA & C: Latin America & Caribbean
- EU & CA: Europe & Central Asia
- AF & ME: Africa & Middle East
- SA: South Asia

- EA & P: East Asia & Pacific
- AN: Antarctica

List of micronations

Many geographically smaller nations are not visible in our global maps due to their size. To make up for this, we selected 15 micronations that are instead prominently highlighted with a circle marker, thus rendering them visible on our maps. We selected these micronations based on their geographic size and the size of their population, as well as their respective role within our digital geographies.

Europe & Central Asia: Malta.

Africa & Middle East: Comoros, Mauritius, Seychelles, São Tomé and Príncipe.

South Asia: Maldives.

East Asia & Pacific: Hong Kong, Marshall Island, Micronesia, Nauru, Palau, Samoa, Singapore, Tonga, Tuvalu.

DATA SOURCES

Geospatial data

World maps and other maps of country boundaries rely on the Cultural Vectors boundary data set provided by Natural Earth (version 4.1.0), which includes boundary data for 247 countries. This free vector map data is placed in the public domain, and available for download at naturalearthdata.com.

World maps are projected with the Equal Earth projection, an equal-area pseudo-cylindrical projection for world maps jointly developed by Bojan Šavrič (Esri), Tom Patterson (US National Park Service) and Bernhard Jenny (Monash University). It was created to provide a visually pleasing alternative to the Gall–Peters projection, which some schools and socially concerned groups have adopted out of concern for fairness. Their priority is to show developing countries in the tropics and developed countries in the north with correctly proportioned sizes. Further information is available at equal-earth.com.

High-resolution population density maps are derived from the Global Human Settlement Layer (GHSL), a high-resolution raster map of global population estimates, generated using new spatial data mining technologies using heterogeneous data, including global archives of fine-scale satellite imagery, census data, and volunteered geographic information. GHSL is supported by the Joint Research Centre (JRC) and the DG for Regional and Urban Policy (DG REGIO) of the European Commission, together with the international partnership GEO Human Planet Initiative. The data is offered under a Creative Commons Attribution 4.0 International licence (CC-BY 4.0), and available for download at ghsl. jrc.ec.europa.eu.

Our maps of Kolkata and Hong Kong include river features and coastline data produced by OpenStreetMap. This data is Copyright 2020 OpenStreetMap contributors. It is available under the Open Database License (ODbL). For more information, see www.openstreetmap.org/copyright.

National and language indicator data

National indicator data is provided by the World Bank as part of the World Bank Open Data repository and their World Development Indicators archive, downloaded in March 2020. This includes data about nation land area and national population estimates, as well as estimates for the national number of broadband subscriptions, and estimates of national internet use in the population. The data is offered under a Creative Commons Attribution 4.0 licence (CC-BY 4.0), and available for download at data.worldbank.org.

Estimates for national language populations are provided by the Unicode Common Locale Data Repository (Unicode CLDR) as a Territory–Language Information data set (version 34b, 2018). The main goal for Unicode language data is to provide approximate figures for the literate, functional population for each language in each territory: that is, the population that is able to read and write each language, and is comfortable enough to use it with computers. The data is Copyright © 1991–2020 Unicode, Inc., and available for download at cldr.unicode.org.

Data about the national cost of broadband connectivity is provided by the International Telecommunications Union (ITU). The data is Copyright © 2017 ITU.

Data about global language speaker populations is provided by Ethnologue: Languages of the World, a database of global languages and their dialects. The data is Copyright © 2019 SIL International.

Online platform indicator data

Statistics about Wikipedia articles and editing activity, including the analysis of geographic locations as denoted by article geotags, are derived from the Wikipedia edit history, downloaded in May 2018 for the 298 language editions available at the time. To reduce storage cost and computational overhead we rely on stub versions of the data, which contains information about article revisions, but does not contain article content. The data is offered under the GNU Free Documentation License (GFDL) and the Creative Commons Attribution-Share-Alike 3.0 License (CC-SA 3.0) and available for download at dumps.wikimedia.org.

Statistics about historic Wikipedia pageviews are provided by the Wikimedia Foundation at stats.wikimedia.org.

OpenStreetMap geographic coverage statistics are derived from a copy of the full OpenStreetMap data set from March 2020. The data is offered under the Open Database share-alike license (ODbL-SA) and available for download at planet.openstreetmap.org.

The GeoNames Gazetteer geographical database is offered under the Creative Commons Attribution 4.0 License (CC-BY 4.0) and available for download at geonames.org.

The iNaturalist database of natural features is made available as GBIF Occurrence Download (10 March 2020). It is offered under the Creative Commons Attribution Non-Commercial 4.0 License (CC BY-NC 4.0) and available for download at gbif.org or https://doi.org/10.15468/dl.sswf1y.

Data about Github open-source code repositories is made available by the GHTorrent project under the Creative Commons Attribution Share-Alike 4.0 License (CC-BY-SA 4.0) and available for download at ghtorrent.org.

Tor Browser usage data is offered under the Creative Commons Attribution 3.0 United States License (CC-BY 3.0 US) and available for download at metrics.torproject.org.

GeoIP lookups to estimate geographic locations for IP addresses contained in these data sets are performed using the GeoLite2 database created by MaxMind, available from maxmind.com.

METHODOLOGY FOR CHAPTER 5

Data collection with automated searches

Our data collection approach seeks to automate the process of imitating a large number of real-world map searches, and collect the search results for further analysis. In principle, Google offers a Places API for ease of automated data access, however we found that its results differ from what is displayed on Google Maps. As we describe in the following sections, we instead execute Google Maps search queries directly (i.e. making website requests that imitate searches by a human user), and collect the structured data that is returned.

Selection of search terms

In this study we seek to investigate Google Maps' coverage of urban affordances, that is, places in the city that may be used as destinations in local navigation. Maybe the canonical example of such a use of the map is the restaurant search, or the related search for 'lunch' or 'dinner'. However, it is not clear what kinds of searches the map supports – while Google Maps in principle accommodates many additional uses, Google unfortunately does not publish statistics about how the map is used in practice. In an attempt to capture a wide range of uses of the map we chose to identify a broad set of urban affordances that are encountered in cities around the world. This includes restaurants, schools, parks and other potential destinations. In order to make a list of such urban affordances we reviewed how such geospatial catalogues are commonly structured. While Google does not publish the content of their geospatial database, they do offer a glimpse of their internal geospatial taxonomy in their public documentation. Specifically, the Google Places API documentation presents a taxonomy of dozens of urban features.[1] We drew further examples of urban affordances from the folksonomy of urban amenities provided by the OpenStreetMap project.[2]

---

1. https://developers.google.com/places/web-service/supported_types.

2. https://wiki.openstreetmap.org/wiki/Map_Features.

We selected a subset of the vocabulary offered by these taxonomies as the basis for our study, informed by multiple considerations:

- We sought to capture a diversity of features to account for the fact that some locations may facilitate certain uses more than others.
- We sought to select a relatively generic vocabulary of such urban features that can be meaningfully applied to a diverse set of cities. For example, we selected more generic categories such as 'museum' rather than more specific terms such as 'museum of modern art'.
- Importantly, we made sure to include a range of urban features that have high spatial density such as shops and schools, while also including public amenities such as parks and universities that may be less frequent within a city, but that are nevertheless commonly found.

The full list of urban features, in alphabetical order, is: atm, bank, bar, cafe, church, coffee, dentist, dinner, florist, food, grocery, hairdresser, hotel, library, lunch, mosque, museum, music, park, pharmacy, place, restaurant, school, shop, supermarket, synagogue, theatre, university. We initially included 'hotel' in this list, but later removed since we repeatedly received error responses when searching for this term in our early trials. We speculate that Google is protecting this particular urban feature as a data set of commercial interest, possibly in response to third parties crawling it for their own commercial purposes. No other search term we tried was affected by such issues.

We further made an attempt to discover parts of the map that are not captured by these basic urban features. To this purpose we additionally include a set of generic nouns and other frequently used words, adopted from an early study of the Google Maps geography (M. Graham and Zook 2013). In alphabetical order, these terms are: cat, christian, democracy, flu, god, government, hindu, internet, jewish, love, monkey, music, muslim, sex, tax, war, wedding. In principle, these generic nouns might help extend the set of locations we can discover, though in practice few of these terms yielded significant volumes of search results.

Translation

We translated these 45 terms into 23 languages, which introduced an additional set of methodological concerns. What a 'correct' translation for a search query is, is a complex matter. For example, one may choose formal or informal terms and phrasings, different alphabets or transliterations, and vary searches in other ways, while still correctly expressing the intended information need. Even the presence of some spelling errors arguably might not invalidate a translation for use in our data collection, since contemporary search engines often accommodate common misspellings. These potential variations are further mediated by the language context, as different languages and writing systems allow for different forms of variation, and admit different forms of error. As a consequence of all these factors, we can expect that different people choose different search terms for the same information need – we might call this the 'searcher's voice'.

We solicited translations for each language by both a professional translation service and volunteer translators, and made use of both sets of translations in our data collection. This simple approach provides us with a degree of confidence in the formal correctness of at least part of the translations, while also allowing for a variety in search strategies and voices. As a minimum we recruited one volunteer translator and one paid translator per language.

Informed by a first round of trial volunteer translations we prepared a detailed briefing for translators where we described the search scenario. We left it up to the translator to select their preferred tone of voice. We asked them to choose search terms that would be used by a native speaker of the respective language, and acknowledged that different people might use different terms for the same information needs.

We selected a professional translator agency specialising in software and website translation, as their translators were familiar with how digital search interfaces are used in practice. We further recruited volunteer translators through our personal networks, either through direct contact or using social media promotion.

Both volunteer and paid translations included instances where translators offered multiple alternative translations per term. We included all these variations in our search corpus. We removed duplicate terms among the submissions, and used the combined set of both translation pools as a basis for our data collection.

Remote data collection

Sampling grid. Our sample searches are organised in spatial grids in order to construct larger regions, rather than just capturing search results at discrete locations. Within each urban region of interest we constructed an even-spaced grid of locations from which to search for local amenities. This sampling grid is constructed from three elements: a centroid for the urban region of interest, a coverage radius to enclose the boundaries of our data collection, and a grid spacing measure to construct the hexagonal search grid.

Our data collection priority was to observe multiple geolinguistically segmented spaces within the same urban region. Although urban centres are likely the most data-dense parts of any urban region, where possible we also wanted to include at least part of each city's suburban ring, as this would allow us to observe potential effects of economic and other demographic divides. Consequently, we constructed search grid boundaries to cover and exceed official city boundaries.

To construct each search grid we first looked up each city's centroid on Wikipedia, where it is stated as a geographic centre. We then selected an appropriate coverage radius to cover most of the inner city and some of the suburbs, using city boundaries as reported by Google Maps as a reference. In many cases, a coverage radius of 10 km was sufficient. In Berlin, a coverage radius of 15 km was necessary to include more of the city's suburban neighbourhoods. The widest coverage radius of 20 km was chosen for São Paulo and Montréal.

The resulting circular area was our basis to construct search grids for every urban region. We sought to achieve a relatively fine spatial resolution for the search grid, where individual search locations were no more than hundreds of meters apart. However, we also sought to complete our data collection process within a period of weeks rather than months, covering dozens of search terms and multiple languages per city. We resolved this trade-off between spatial resolution and collection effort by limiting each city's grid to hundreds or at most low thousands of search locations.

We constructed individual search locations within the coverage radius using the hexagonal spatial grid library H3 (Bondaruk, Roberts and Robertson 2019). We chose H3 as a reference as it offers a standardised global grid at even-spaced distances across multiple spatial scales. For most cities we selected H3's scale 8 as a basis, which offers a grid spacing of 460 m between individual sample points. Berlin's 15 km coverage radius yields around 1,400 sample points at this scale, while a higher-resolution grid in H3's scale 9 would require an order of magnitude more samples, at 170 m grid spacing. We chose the coarser scale 7 at 1.2 km grid spacing for Montréal and São Paulo, which span vast regions, and for Nairobi, where we simply sought to collect enough data to illustrate its geography in broad terms.

In total, just over 9,000 sample points were used to organise data collection across the eleven cities. For our confirmatory analysis we constructed a global grid using H3's scale 2, at an average grid spacing of approximately 160 km, resulting in 2,616 sample points over land.

Scraping. Data collection began in November 2019 and took approximately two months. We executed Google Maps searches at every sample point, sending a search request for the translated search term in each region's languages of interest. In total, we executed 2 million search queries across the eleven urban regions, and 1.5 million searches across our global search grid.

In our attempt to mimic the human search experience, for every search query in a particular language we also state that we want the results to be presented in this language, using a Google Maps facility to select user interface languages. This ensures that, for example, a French-language search will yield French-language results, even if it is a search in a location where French is not an official language.

For each search we collected the top 400 search results, if available, in an attempt to crawl the contents of Google's geospatial database as extensively as possible. However, for certain analyses we only consider the top 20 results, analogous to the first page of search results on the Google Maps website.

We made these requests with a custom crawler software, running on a single machine located in the UK. The crawler sent a user agent string that imitated a desktop browser. To avoid throttling or getting blocked we alternated between multiple fresh session cookies between requests, and data was collected with a delay of approximately one second between requests. The data collection process was largely uneventful. A brief Google Maps service outage resulted in a single failed request which was later repeated, but otherwise all requests received successful responses.

Preparing for analysis. The entries in each search result listing provided us with information about the locations known to Google Maps. The metadata for each individual search result entry contains a full description of the respective location or venue. It includes a name for the location or venue, a homepage URL if available, a set of category labels, a geographic location as both geographic coordinates as well as a street address, and a unique identifier code (a hex-encoded 16-byte number that is unique to the location or venue). To prepare the data for analysis, we computed the great-circle distance (or Haversine distance) between each search result and the respective search location from which it was discovered.

Each search result entry further includes an identifier code for the result language, that is, an automated assessment of the language in which the search result is described. This allowed us to observe whether the result language matched the language of our search request. This is a nuanced comparison, as the language identifier codes reported by Google allow for many regional and linguistic variants of particular languages. Our primary concern was whether someone searching in a particular language would be able to interpret a search result without having to switch languages. Consequently, after review of the language codes reported in search results, we chose to conflate certain language variants, so that Swiss and Austrian variants of German are considered to be equivalent to German, South American variants of Spanish equivalent to Spanish, Brazilian Portuguese equivalent to Portuguese, and Canadian French equivalent to French. We further consider Singaporean Chinese a mutually intelligible form of Mandarin, and Hong Kong and Malaysian Chinese as mutually intelligible forms of Cantonese. Finally, latin-script transliterations of Hebrew- and Russian-language results are considered equivalent to these languages in their native scripts.

Limitations

Any attempt at a comparison at global scale brings with it some intrinsic and insurmountable challenges. Importantly, it requires us to account for many dimensions of difference involving aspects of urban geography, information environments and language culture, much of which we can only observe to a limited extent. In other words, any global analysis is rich in unknown unknowns. This observation is recurrent throughout our book, and it prompts us to acknowledge the impossibility of studying human activity at global scale. Fundamentally, it brings with it all the problems of trying to force the complexities of human existence into a positivist framework of quantifiable evidence. As we have discussed in the opening section of Chapter 4, rather than taking any numbers at face value we have to accept that we are faced with significant uncertainties in our observations, and that we need to remain careful about what claims we can reasonably make. At the very least we need to be prepared to answer some common critiques of our approach. In the following sections we discuss some of the central concerns, and how we sought to address them.

No personalisation. We make no attempt to model personalisation effects (i.e. DEFINE), and cannot assess to what extent our search results are also informed by behavioural profiling and recommender systems. We started our data collection with new session cookies. It is unclear whether this was even necessary, as recent work on Google Maps search result personalisation has illustrated: in a comparative study across multiple locations, Smets, Montero and Ballon (2019) found that search results varied significantly between different search languages, while there was only a comparatively small personalisation effect. To confirm this, we manually replicated a subset of our searches with a personal account that is subject to personalisation, and found that results broadly matched those from our automated data collection.

Not an exhaustive study. We want to emphasise that this is not an attempt at an exhaustive study, which would be infeasible at the vast scale of Google Maps without having access to the underlying geospatial database. Instead, it is an attempt to present a diverse set of urban case studies complemented with a high-level global overview, which taken together can give us a richer understanding of the extent and limits of Google Maps as a map of the world.

Furthermore, we have already discussed in our discussion of findings in Chapter 5 that we were unable to include several large cities that would complement the global picture in important ways, either because they were not officially supported by the platform and consequently absent on the map, or because we failed to recruit the requisite number of translators and translations. This affects many African and South American languages, and many of the world's indigenous languages which unfortunately are not represented in this study. This is illustrated by the fact that despite our best efforts, we failed to recruit enough translators to achieve a full translation for Guaraní. This exclusion in itself is already noteworthy, as it illustrates how frequently instances of existing exclusion lead to further exclusion. We would have liked for many more places and peoples to be recognised in our study, but our efforts rely on the availability of particular capacities and other forms of support.

As a result, we also have to acknowledge that this restricts the generalisability of our findings: we can only study places and languages that are already represented in some form. In other words, we have to acknowledge that this is a study of the privileged few – which may be inevitable in any such study of 'unknown unknowns'.

Cultural assumptions embedded in our study design. At the core of our study design is a list of search terms, a catalogue of urban features that we curated from existing geospatial taxonomies. This list was selected with some care, and is the result of several rounds of discussion and reflection. And yet, the process involved a set of normative assumptions that may not be globally universal. Most importantly, to an extent our study inherits the prior cultural assumptions embedded in the geospatial taxonomies we relied on. As a consequence, we are likely to miss issues involving urban phenomena that are fully outside our own cultural frame. For example, it is noteworthy that we started with an English-centric vocabulary of urban features. By comparison, translators for Chinese dialects reported that common food and restaurant vocabulary in these languages is often more nuanced and more specific than the broad English categories of 'lunch' or 'dinner'.

Secondly, our study design relies on a basic set of assumptions about how the map is used. Google does not share information about how people navigate their map in practice, and as a consequence it is not clear to what extent our data collection approach reflects actual search behaviour, and whether this might vary across global locations. For example, it is not documented what search terms are used, whether people ask full-sentence questions or search for keywords, and to what degree this differs between languages and locations.

Bibliography

Agha, Zena. 2020. 'Maps, Technology, and Decolonial Spatial Practices in Palestine'. Al-Shabaka, The Palestinian Policy Network. https://al-shabaka. org/briefs/maps-technology-and-decolonial-spatial-practices-in-palestine/.

Ali, Syed Mustafa. 2016. 'A Brief Introduction to Decolonial Computing'. *XRDS: Crossroads, The ACM Magazine for Students* 22(4): 16–21.

Anwar, Mohammad Amir and Mark Graham. 2020. 'Between a Rock and a Hard Place: Freedom, Flexibility, Precarity and Vulnerability in the Gig Economy in Africa'. *Competition & Change*, 1024529420914473.

Arora, Payal. 2019. *The Next Billion Users: Digital Life beyond the West*. Harvard University Press.

Ash, J., R. Kitchin and A. Leszczynski (2016) 'Digital Turn, Digital Geographies?' *Progress in Human Geography* 42(1): 25–43.

Ballatore, Andrea, Mark Graham and Shilad Sen. 2017. 'Digital Hegemonies: The Localness of Search Engine Results'. *Annals of the American Association of Geographers* 107(5): 1194–1215.

Barlow, J.P. *A Declaration of the Independence of Cyberspace*. Vol. 2009. 19 May 1996. Davos, Switzerland. http://homes.eff.org/ barlow/Declaration-Final. html.

Barnett, D. 2018. 'Can We Trust Wikipedia? 1.4 Billion People Can't Be Wrong'. *The Independent*, 2018. www.independent.co.uk/news/long_reads/wikipedia-explained-what-it-trustworthy-how-work-wikimedia-2030-a8213446.html.

Barthes, R. 1980. 'The Plates of the Encyclopedia'. In *New Critical Essays*, 27. Hill and Wang.

Battelle, John. 2016. 'The Waze Effect: AI & The Public Commons'. *NewCo Shift* (blog). 2016. https://medium.com/newco/the-waze-effect-ai-the-public-commons-d3926fce108e.

Benjamin, Ruha. 2019. 'Race after Technology: Abolitionist Tools for the New Jim Code'. *Social Forces*.

Benkler, Yochai. 2002. 'Coase's Penguin, or, Linux and "The Nature of the Firm"'. *Yale Law Journal*, 369–446.

——. 2006. *The Wealth of Networks: How Social Production Transforms Markets and Freedom*. Yale University Press.

Bensinger, G. 2020. 'Google Redraws the Borders on Maps Depending on Who's Looking'. *The Washington Post*, 2020. www.washingtonpost.com/technology/2020/02/14/google-maps-political-borders/.

Bittner, Christian. 2017. 'OpenStreetMap in Israel and Palestine – "Game Changer" or Reproducer of Contested Cartographies?' *Political Geography* 57: 34–48.

Bondaruk, B, S.A. Roberts and C. Robertson. 2019. 'Discrete Global Grid Systems: Operational Capability of the Current State of the Art'. In *Proceedings of the 7th Conference on Spatial Knowledge and Information Canada (SKI2019)*. Vol. 2323.

Boy, John D. and Justus Uitermark. 2015. 'Capture and Share the City: Mapping Instagram's Uneven Geography in Amsterdam'. In *Conference 'The Ideal City Between Myth and Reality. Representations, Policies, Contradictions and Challenges for Tomorrows Urban Life'*, Urbino. Vol. 27.

——. 2017. 'Reassembling the City through Instagram'. *Transactions of the Institute of British Geographers* 42(4): 612–624.

Brown, Tom B., Benjamin Mann, Nick Ryder, Melanie Subbiah, Jared Kaplan, Prafulla Dhariwal, Arvind Neelakantan et al. 2020. *Language Models Are Few-Shot Learners*. ArXiv, Cornell University.

Brunet-Jailly, E. (Ed.). 2015. *Border Disputes: A Global Encyclopedia*. ABC-CLIO.

Bruns, Axel. 2008. *Blogs, Wikipedia, Second Life, and Beyond: From Production to Produsage*. Vol. 45. Peter Lang.

Budhathoki, Nama R. 2010. 'Participants' Motivations to Contribute Geographic Information in an Online Community'. PhD thesis, University of Illinois at Urbana-Champaign.

Budhathoki, Nama R. and Caroline Haythornthwaite. 2013. 'Motivation for Open Collaboration: Crowd and Community Models and the Case of OpenStreetMap'. *American Behavioral Scientist* 57(5): 548–575.

Buolamwini, Joy and Timnit Gebru. 2018. 'Gender Shades: Intersectional Accuracy Disparities in Commercial Gender Classification'. In *Conference on Fairness, Accountability and Transparency*, 77–91.

Carraro, Valentina. 2019. 'Grounding the Digital: A Comparison of Waze "Avoid Dangerous Areas" Feature in Jerusalem, Rio de Janeiro and the US'. *GeoJournal*, 1–19.

Carraro, Valentina and Bart Wissink. 2018. 'Participation and Marginality on the Geoweb: The Politics of Non-Mapping on OpenStreetMap Jerusalem'. *Geoforum* 90: 64–73.

Castells, Manuel. 1999. *Information Technology, Globalization and Social Development*. 114. UNRISD, Geneva.

——. 2010. 'Globalisation, Networking, Urbanisation: Reflections on the Spatial Dynamics of the Information Age'. *Urban Studies* 47(13): 2737–2745.

Choi, Boreum, Kira Alexander, Robert E. Kraut and John M. Levine. 2010. 'Socialization Tactics in Wikipedia and Their Effects'. In *Proceedings of the 2010 ACM Conference on Computer Supported Cooperative Work*, 107–116.

Ciampaglia, Giovanni Luca and Dario Taraborelli. 2015. 'MoodBar: Increasing New User Retention in Wikipedia through Lightweight Socialization'. In *Proceedings of the 18th ACM Conference on Computer Supported Cooperative Work & Social Computing*, 734–742.

Clark, Liat. 2014. 'The Race to Contain West Africa's Ebola Outbreak'. *Wired U.K.*, 2014. www.wired.co.uk/article/ebola-open-street-map.

Clary, E. Gil, Mark Snyder, Robert D. Ridge, John Copeland, Arthur A. Stukas, Julie Haugen and Peter Miene. 1998. 'Understanding and Assessing the

Motivations of Volunteers: A Functional Approach'. *Journal of Personality and Social Psychology* 74(6): 1516.

Collins, Katie. 2013. 'Uncharted Territory: The Power of Amateur Cartographers'. *Wired*, 2013. www.wired.com/2013/08/power-of-amateur-cartographers/.

Cosgrove, Denis. 1999. 'Global Illumination and Enlightenment in the Geographies of Vincenzo Coronelli and Athanasius Kircher'. In *Geography and Enlightenment*, eds David Livingstone and Charles Withers, 33–66. The University of Chicago Press.

Costanza-Chock, Sasha. 2020. *Design Justice: Community-Led Practices to Build the Worlds We Need*. MIT Press.

Crampton, Jeremy W. 2008. 'Will Peasants Map? Hyperlinks, Map Mashups, and the Future of Information'. *The Hyperlinked Society: Questioning Connections in a Digital Age*, ed. J. Turow and L. Tsui, 206–26. University of Michigan Press.

Crang, Mike. 1996. 'Envisioning Urban Histories: Bristol as Palimpsest, Postcards, and Snapshots'. *Environment and Planning A* 28(3): 429–452.

Cresci, Elena. 2016. 'Google Maps Accused of Deleting Palestine – but the Truth is More Complicated'. *The Guardian*.

Dawson, Stella. 2014. 'Online Volunteers Map Uncharted Ebola Zones to Help Save Lives'. *Thomson Reuters Foundation*, 2014. https://news.trust.org/item/20140918050913-ho2mk/.

Dean, David. 2017. 'Accelerating the Digital Economy in the Middle East, North Africa and Turkey'. Internet Corporation for Assigned Names and Numbers (ICANN).

Devriendt, Lomme, Andrew Boulton, Stanley Brunn, Ben Derudder and Frank Witlox. 2011. 'Searching for Cyberspace: The Position of Major Cities in the Information Age'. *Journal of Urban Technology* 18(1): 73–92.

Dewey, Caitlin. 2019. 'How Google's Bad Data Wiped a Neighborhood off the Map'. *Medium*, 2019. https://onezero.medium.com/how-googles-bad-data-wiped-a-neighborhood-off-the-map-80c4c13f1c2b.

Dittus, Martin and Licia Capra. 2017. 'Private Peer Feedback as Engagement Driver in Humanitarian Mapping'. *Proceedings of the ACM on Human-Computer Interaction* 1 (CSCW): 1–18.

Dittus, Martin and Mark Graham. 2019. 'Mapping Wikipedia's Geolinguistic Contours'. *Digital Culture & Society* 5(1): 147–164.

Dittus, Martin, Giovanni Quattrone and Licia Capra. 2016a. 'Analysing Volunteer Engagement in Humanitarian Mapping: Building Contributor Communities at Large Scale'. In *Proceedings of the 19th ACM Conference on Computer-Supported Cooperative Work & Social Computing*, 108–118.

——. 2016b. 'Social Contribution Settings and Newcomer Retention in Humanitarian Crowd Mapping'. In *International Conference on Social Informatics*, 179–193. Springer.

——. 2017. 'Mass Participation during Emergency Response: Event-Centric Crowdsourcing in Humanitarian Mapping'. In *Proceedings of the 2017 ACM Conference on Computer Supported Cooperative Work and Social Computing*, 1290–1303.

Dodge, Martin and Rob Kitchin. 2005. 'Code and the Transduction of Space'. *Annals of the Association of American Geographers* 95(1): 162–180.

——. 2007. '"Outlines of a World Coming into Existence": Pervasive Computing and the Ethics of Forgetting'. *Environment and Planning B: Planning and Design* 34(3): 431–445.

D'Onfro, Jilian. 2016. 'Google Maps is the "Swiss Army Knife" of the Company's Smart Assistant Future'. *Business Insider*, 2016. www.businessinsider.com/jen-fitzpatrick-on-google-maps-2016-9.

Eberhard, David M., Gary F. Simons and Charles D. Fennig. 2020. *Ethnologue: Languages of the World*, 23rd edition. SIL International. www.ethnologue.com/.

Eide, Elisabeth. 2016. 'Strategic Essentialism'. In *The Wiley Blackwell Encyclopedia of Gender and Sexuality Studies*, 1–2. Wiley-Blackwell.

El-Essawi, Raghda. 2011. 'Arabic in Latin Script in Egypt: Who Uses It and Why'. In *Global English and Arabic: Issues of Language, Culture, and Identity*, 253–284, ed. Ahmad Al-Issa and Laila S. Dahan. Peter Lang.

Elwood, S. 2006. 'Critical Issues in Participatory GIS: Deconstructions, Reconstructions, and New Research Directions'. *Transactions in GIS* 10(5): 693–708.

Elwood, Sarah and Agnieszka Leszczynski. 2013. 'New Spatial Media, New Knowledge Politics'. *Transactions of the Institute of British Geographers* 38(4): 544–559.

Escobar, Arturo. 2018. *Designs for the Pluriverse: Radical Interdependence, Autonomy, and the Making of Worlds*. Duke University Press.

Faccio, Mara and John J. McConnell. 2017. 'Death by Pokémon GO: The Economic and Human Cost of Using Apps While Driving'. *Journal of Risk and Insurance*.

Floridi, Luciano. 2014. *The Fourth Revolution: How the Infosphere Is Reshaping Human Reality*. Oxford University Press.

Foderaro, Lisa W. 2017. 'Navigation Apps Are Turning Quiet Neighborhoods into Traffic Nightmares'. *The New York Times*. www.nytimes.com/2017/12/24/nyregion/traffic-apps-gps-neighborhoods.html.

Ford, Heather. 2015. 'Fact Factories: Wikipedia and the Power to Represent'. PhD thesis, University of Oxford.

Ford, Heather, Shilad Sen, David R. Musicant and Nathaniel Miller. 2013. 'Getting to the Source: Where Does Wikipedia Get Its Information From?' In *Proceedings of the 9th International Symposium on Open Collaboration*, 1–10.

Foucault, Michel. 2000. *Power*, ed. James D. Faubion, trans. Robert Hurley et al. New Press.

Friederici, Nicolas, Sanna Ojanperä and Mark Graham. 2017. 'The Impact of Connectivity in Africa: Grand Visions and the Mirage of Inclusive Digital Development'. *The Electronic Journal of Information Systems in Developing Countries* 79(1): 1–20.

Gallert, Peter, Heike Winschiers-Theophilus, Gereon K. Kapuire, Colin Stanley, Daniel G. Cabrero and Bobby Shabangu. 2016. 'Indigenous Knowledge for Wikipedia: A Case Study with an OvaHerero Community in Eastern Namibia'.

In *Proceedings of the First African Conference on Human Computer Interaction*, 155–159.

Garcia, David. 2020. 'One More Map'. *How to Map an Island in the Pacific* (blog). 2020. https://tinyletter.com/mapmakerdavid/letters/one-more-map.

Garfield, Simon. 2012. *On the Map: Why the World Looks the Way It Does*. Profile Books.

Geiger, R. Stuart and Aaron Halfaker. 2013. 'Using Edit Sessions to Measure Participation in Wikipedia'. In *Proceedings of the 2013 Conference on Computer Supported Cooperative Work*, 861–870.

Glott, Ruediger, Philipp Schmidt and Rishab Ghosh. 2010. 'Wikipedia Survey–Overview of Results'. *United Nations University: Collaborative Creativity Group* 8: 1158–1178.

Google. 2017. 'Google Map Maker Has Closed'. *Google Support* (blog). 2017. https://support.google.com/mapmaker/answer/7195127.

——. 2020. 'About Google'. 2020. https://about.google.

Goss, J. 1995. 'We Know Who You Are and We Know Where You Live: The Instrumental Rationality of Geodemographic Systems'. *Economic Geography* 71: 171–198.

Graells-Garrido, Eduardo, Leo Ferres, Diego Caro and Loreto Bravo. 2017. 'The Effect of Pokémon Go on the Pulse of the City: A Natural Experiment'. *EPJ Data Science* 6(1): 1–19.

Graham, Mark. 2010. 'Neogeography and the Palimpsests of Place: Web 2.0 and the Construction of a Virtual Earth'. *Tijdschrift Voor Economische En Sociale Geografie* 101(4): 422 436.

——. 2018. 'The Virtual Palimpsest of the Global City Network'. In *The Globalizing Cities Reader*, eds X. Ren and R. Keil, 198–204. Routledge.

——. 2020. 'A Robot Wrote This Entire Article. Are You Scared Yet, Human?' *The Guardian*, 2020. www.theguardian.com/commentisfree/2020/sep/08/robot-wrote-this-article-gpt-3.

Graham, Mark, Stefano De Sabbata and Matthew A. Zook. 2015. 'Towards a Study of Information Geographies: (Im)Mutable Augmentations and a Mapping of the Geographies of Information'. *Geo: Geography and Environment* 2(1): 88–105.

Graham, Mark and Martin Dittus. 2018. 'To Reduce Inequality, Wikipedia Should Consider Paying Editors'. *Wired*, 2018. www.wired.co.uk/article/wikipedia-inequality-pay-editors.

Graham, Mark, Scott Hale and Monica Stephens. 2011. *Geographies of the World's Knowledge*. Oxford Internet Institute.

Graham, Mark and Bernie Hogan. 2014. 'Uneven Openness: Barriers to MENA Representation on Wikipedia'. *IDRC Project Technical Report*.

Graham, Mark, Bernie Hogan, Ralph K. Straumann and Ahmed Medhat. 2014. 'Uneven Geographies of User-Generated Information: Patterns of Increasing Informational Poverty'. *Annals of the Association of American Geographers* 104(4): 746–764. https://doi.org/10.1080/00045608.2014.910087.

Graham, Mark, Ralph K. Straumann and Bernie Hogan. 2015. 'Digital Divisions of Labor and Informational Magnetism: Mapping Participation in Wikipedia'. *Annals of the Association of American Geographers* 105(6): 1158–1178.

Graham, Mark and Matthew Zook. 2013. 'Augmented Realities and Uneven Geographies: Exploring the Geolinguistic Contours of the Web'. *Environment and Planning A* 45(1): 77–99.

Graham, Mark, Matthew Zook and Andrew Boulton. 2013. 'Augmented Reality in Urban Places: Contested Content and the Duplicity of Code'. *Transactions of the Institute of British Geographers* 38(3): 464–479.

Graham, Stephen. 1998. 'The End of Geography or the Explosion of Place? Conceptualizing Space, Place and Information Technology'. *Progress in Human Geography* 22(2): 165–185.

Graham, Stephen D.N. 2005. 'Software-Sorted Geographies'. *Progress in Human Geography* 29(5): 562–580.

Gramsci, Antonio. 1971. 'Hegemony'. In *Selections from the Prison Notebooks*. International Publishers.

Haggan, Madeline. 2007. 'Text Messaging in Kuwait. Is the Medium the Message?' *Multilingua* 26(4): 427–449.

Haklay, Mordechai and Patrick Weber. 2008. 'Openstreetmap: User-Generated Street Maps'. *IEEE Pervasive Computing* 7(4): 12–18.

Haklay, Muki and Nama R. Budhathoki. 2010. 'OpenStreetMap – Overview and Motivational Factors'. http://hdl.handle.net/2142/16461.

Halfaker, Aaron, R. Stuart Geiger, Jonathan T. Morgan and John Riedl. 2013. 'The Rise and Decline of an Open Collaboration System: How Wikipedia's Reaction to Popularity Is Causing Its Decline'. *American Behavioral Scientist* 57(5): 664–688.

Hanrahan, Benjamin V., Ning F. Ma and Chien Wen Yuan. 2018. 'The Roots of Bias on Uber'. *ArXiv Preprint ArXiv:1803.08579*.

Harley, J.B. 1989. 'Deconstructing the Map'. *Cartographica* 26(2): 1–20.

He, Shiqing, Allen Yilun Lin, Eytan Adar and Brent Hecht. 2018. 'The_Tower_of_Babel. Jpg: Diversity of Visual Encyclopedic Knowledge Across Wikipedia Language Editions'. In *Twelfth International AAAI Conference on Web and Social Media*.

Hecht, Brent Jaron. 2013. 'The Mining and Application of Diverse Cultural Perspectives in User-Generated Content'. PhD thesis, Northwestern University.

Hetoevehotohke'e Lucchesi, Annita. 2020. 'Spatial Data and (De) Colonization: Incorporating Indigenous Data Sovereignty Principles into Cartographic Research'. *Cartographica: The International Journal for Geographic Information and Geovisualization* 55(3): 163–169.

Hill, Benjamin Mako. 2013. 'Almost Wikipedia: Eight Early Encyclopedia Projects and the Mechanisms of Collective Action'. *Massachusetts Institute of Technology*, 1–38.

Hinnosaar, Marit, Toomas Hinnosaar, Michael E. Kummer and Olga Slivko. 2019. 'Wikipedia Matters'. Available at: SSRN 3046400.

HOT. 2020a. 'HOT Community Grants'. 2020. www.hotosm.org/community/community-grants/.

——. 2020b. 'HOT Tasking Manager'. 2020. https://tasks.hotosm.org.

Howard, Dorothy. 2014. 'Thoughts on Wikipedia Editing and Digital Labour'. https://en.wikipedia.org/wiki/Wikipedia:Thoughts_on_Wikipedia_Editing_and_Digital_Labor.

Howe, Jeff. 2006. 'The Rise of Crowdsourcing'. *Wired*, 2006. www.wired.com/2006/06/crowds/.

Ibarz, Julian. 2017. 'Updating Google Maps with Deep Learning and Street View'. *Google AI Blog* (blog). 2017. https://ai.googleblog.com/2017/05/updating-google-maps-with-deep-learning.html.

ITU. 2017. 'ICT Prices, 2017'. International Telecommunication Union.

Jeffries, Arianne and Leon Yin. 2020. 'Google's Top Search Result? Surprise! It's Google'. *The Markup*, 2020. https://themarkup.org/google-the-giant/2020/07/28/google-search-results-prioritize-google-products-over-competitors.

Jenkins, Henry. 2006. *Fans, Bloggers, and Gamers: Exploring Participatory Culture*. NYU Press.

Karimi, Fariba, Ludvig Bohlin, Anna Samoilenko, Martin Rosvall and Andrea Lancichinetti. 2015. 'Mapping Bilateral Information Interests Using the Activity of Wikipedia Editors'. *Palgrave Communications* 1(1). https://doi.org/10.1057/palcomms.2015.41.

Katz, Rachel. 2018. 'More than a Dating App'. School of Social Sciences, University of Manchester (blog), 2018. www.socialsciences.manchester.ac.uk/about/stories/dating-app/.

Keegan, Brian, Darren Gergle and Noshir Contractor. 2013. 'Hot Off the Wiki: Structures and Dynamics of Wikipedia's Coverage of Breaking News Events'. *American Behavioral Scientist* 57(5): 595–622.

Kitchin, Rob. 2011. 'The Programmable City'. *Environment and Planning B: Planning and Design* 38(6): 945–951.

——. 2014. 'Big Data, New Epistemologies and Paradigm Shifts'. *Big Data & Society* 1(1): 2053951714528481.

Kittur, Aniket, Bongwon Suh, Bryan A. Pendleton and Ed H. Chi. 2007. 'He Says, She Says: Conflict and Coordination in Wikipedia'. In *Proceedings of the SIGCHI Conference on Human Factors in Computing Systems*, 453–462.

Koh, Joon, Young-Gul Kim, Brian Butler and Gee-Woo Bock. 2007. 'Encouraging Participation in Virtual Communities'. *Communications of the ACM* 50(2): 68–73.

Konieczny, Piotr. 2018. 'Volunteer Retention, Burnout and Dropout in Online Voluntary Organizations: Stress, Conflict and Retirement of Wikipedians'. In *Research in Social Movements, Conflicts and Change (Research in Social Movements, Conflicts and Change, Volume 42)*, 199–219. Emerald Publishing.

Kraut, Robert E. and Paul Resnick. 2012. *Building Successful Online Communities: Evidence-Based Social Design*. MIT Press.

Kwak, Haewoon, Jisun An, Joni Salminen, Soon-Gyo Jung and Bernard J. Jansen. 2018. 'What We Read, What We Search: Media Attention and Public Attention among 193 Countries'. In *Proceedings of the 2018 World Wide Web Conference*, 893–902.

Kyriakoullis, Leantros and Panayiotis Zaphiris. 2016. 'Culture and HCI: A Review of Recent Cultural Studies in HCI and Social Networks'. *Universal Access in the Information Society* 15(4): 629–642.

Laclau, Ernesto and Chantal Mouffe. 1985. *Hegemony and Socialist Strategy*. Verso.

Lam, Shyong (Tony) K., Anuradha Uduwage, Zhenhua Dong, Shilad Sen, David R. Musicant, Loren Terveen and John Riedl. 2011. 'WP:Clubhouse? An Exploration of Wikipedia's Gender Imbalance'. In *Proceedings of the 7th International Symposium on Wikis and Open Collaboration*, 1–10.

Langley, Paul and Andrew Leyshon. 2016. 'Platform Capitalism: The Intermediation and Capitalisation of Digital Economic Circulation'. *Finance and Society*, 1–21.

Latour, Bruno. 1986. 'Visualization and Cognition'. *Knowledge and Society* 6(6): 1–40.

Lechner, Marco. 2011. 'Nutzungspotentiale Crowdsource-Erhobener Geodaten Auf Verschiedenen Skalen'. PhD thesis, Universitätsbibliothek Freiburg.

Lefebvre, Henri. 1991. *Critique of Everyday Life: Foundations for a Sociology of the Everyday*. Vol. 2. Verso.

Lemmerich, Florian, Diego Sáez-Trumper, Robert West and Leila Zia. 2019. 'Why the World Reads Wikipedia: Beyond English Speakers'. In *Proceedings of the Twelfth ACM International Conference on Web Search and Data Mining*, 618–626.

Lessig, Lawrence. 2003. 'An Information Society: Free or Feudal'. www.itu.int/wsis/docs/pc2/visionaries/lessig.pdf.

Leszczynski, Agnieszka. 2012. 'Situating the Geoweb in Political Economy'. *Progress in Human Geography* 36(1): 72–89.

——. 2015. 'Spatial Media/Tion'. *Progress in Human Geography* 39(6): 729–751.

Lin, Cindy. 2020. 'How to Make a Forest'. *E-Flux*, 2020. www.e-flux.com/architecture/at-the-border/325757/how-to-make-a-forest/.

Lin, Yu-Wei. 2011. 'A Qualitative Enquiry into OpenStreetMap Making'. *New Review of Hypermedia and Multimedia* 17(1): 53–71.

Livingstone, David. 1992. *The Geographical Tradition: Episodes in the History of a Contested Enterprise*. Blackwell.

Lorini, Valerio, Javier Rando, Diego Saez-Trumper and Carlos Castillo. 2020. 'Uneven Coverage of Natural Disasters in Wikipedia: The Case of Flood'. *ArXiv Preprint ArXiv:2001.08810*.

Madrigal, Alexis C. 2012. 'How Google Builds Its Maps – and What It Means for the Future of Everything'. *The Atlantic*, 2012. www.theatlantic.com/technology/archive/2012/09/how-google-builds-its-maps-and-what-it-means-for-the-future-of-everything/261913/.

Mak, Aaron. 2018. 'Can You Trust Waze During an Emergency Like the California Wildfires'. *Slate*, 2018. www.slate.com/blogs/future_tense/2017/12/07/california_wildfires_raise_questions_about_whether_you_can_trust_waze_google.html.

Malecki, Edward J. 2002. 'The Economic Geography of the Internet's Infrastructure'. *Economic Geography* 78(4): 399–424.

Marr, Bernard. 2017. 'Where Can You Buy Big Data? Here Are the Biggest Consumer Data Brokers'. *Forbes*, 2017.

Martin, Zak. 2016. 'Google: Put Palestine on Your Maps!' *Change.org*, 2016. www.change.org/p/google-inc-google-put-palestine-on-your-maps.

Massey, Doreen. 2005. *For Space*. SAGE.

McCulloch, Gretchen. 2019. 'Coding Is for Everyone – as Long as You Speak English'. *Wired*, 2019. www.wired.com/story/coding-is-for-everyoneas-long-as-you-speak-english/.

McGurk, Thomas J. and Sébastien Caquard. 2020. 'To What Extent Can Online Mapping Be Decolonial? A Journey throughout Indigenous Cartography in Canada'. *The Canadian Geographer/Le Géographe Canadien* 64(1): 49–64.

McMahon, Connor, Isaac Johnson and Brent Hecht. 2017. 'The Substantial Interdependence of Wikipedia and Google: A Case Study on the Relationship between Peer Production Communities and Information Technologies'. In *Eleventh International AAAI Conference on Web and Social Media*.

Meyer, Robinson. 2015. 'The Internet Mapmakers Helping Nepal'. *The Atlantic*, 2015. www.theatlantic.com/technology/archive/2015/05/the-mapmakers-helping-nepal/392228/.

Mignolo, Walter. 2013. 'On Pluriversality'. *Walter Mignolo* 30: 1–7.

Miller, Greg. 2014. 'The Huge, Unseen Operation Behind the Accuracy of Google Maps', 2014. www.wired.com/2014/12/google-maps-ground-truth/.

Mitchell, Timothy. 2002. *Rule of Experts*. University of California Press.

Monmonier, Mark. 1996. *How to Lie With Maps*. University of Chicago Press.

Moss, P. and K.F. Al-Hindi. 2007. *Feminisms in Geography: Rethinking Space, Place, and Knowledges*. Rowman & Littlefield.

Nagel, T. 1986. *The View from Nowhere*. Oxford University Press.

Nederman, C.J., B.S. Jones and L. Fitzgerald. 1998. 'Lost in Cyberspace: Democratic Prospects of Computer-Mediated Communication'. *Contemporary Politics* 4(1): 9–21.

Neis, Pascal and Dennis Zielstra. 2014. 'Recent Developments and Future Trends in Volunteered Geographic Information Research: The Case of OpenStreetMap'. *Future Internet* 6(1): 76–106.

Noble, Safiya Umoja. 2018. *Algorithms of Oppression: How Search Engines Reinforce Racism*. NYU Press.

Norman, Don. 2013. *The Design of Everyday Things: Revised and Expanded Edition*. Basic Books.

Nov, Oded. 2007. 'What Motivates Wikipedians?' *Communications of the ACM* 50(11): 60–64.

O'Beirne, Justin. 2017. 'The Google Maps Moat'. 2017. www.justinobeirne.com/google-maps-moat.

Ortega, Felipe. 2009. 'Wikipedia: A Quantitative Analysis'. PhD thesis, Universidad Rey Juan Carlos, Madrid.

OSMF. 2018. 'OSM Condemns Recent Anti-Semitic Vandalism'. 2018. https://blog.openstreetmap.org/2018/08/30/osm-condemns-vandalism/.

Oxford English Dictionary. 2015. 'Information, n.'. www.oed.com/view dictionaryentry/Entry/95568.

Parikh, Bobby. 2012. 'Expanded Coverage of Building Footprints in Google Maps'. *Google Blog* (blog), 2012. https://maps.googleblog.com/2012/10/expanded-coverage-of-building.html.

Pedersen, Jay, David Kocsis, Abhishek Tripathi, Alvin Tarrell, Aruna Weerakoon, Nargess Tahmasbi, Jie Xiong, Wei Deng, Onook Oh and Gert-Jan De Vreede. 2013. 'Conceptual Foundations of Crowdsourcing: A Review of IS Research'. In *2013 46th Hawaii International Conference on System Sciences*, 579–588. IEEE.

Pentzold, Christian. 2009. 'Fixing the Floating Gap: The Online Encyclopaedia Wikipedia as a Global Memory Place'. *Memory Studies* 2(2): 255–272.

Perkins, Chris. 2014. 'Plotting Practices and Politics: (Im)Mutable Narratives in OpenStreetMap'. *Transactions of the Institute of British Geographers* 39(2): 304–317.

Pickles, John. 1995. *Ground Truth: The Social Implications of Geographic Information Systems*. Guilford Press.

——. 2004. *A History of Spaces: Cartographic Reason, Mapping, and the Geo-Coded World*. Psychology Press.

Pratt, Mary Louise. 1992. *Imperial Eyes*. Routledge.

Radford, Tyler. 2020. 'Haiti 10 Years Later: Growth of a Humanitarian Mapping Community'. 2020. www.hotosm.org/updates/haiti-10-years-later-growth-of-a-crisis-mapping-community/.

Raish, Michael. 2019. 'Identifying and Classifying Harassment in Arabic Wikipedia: A "Netnography"'. Wikimedia Foundation.

Reagle, Joseph. 2012. '"410 Gone": Infocide in Open Content Communities'. Available at: SSRN 2362301.

Richardson, Lizzie. 2020. 'Coordinating the City: Platforms as Flexible Spatial Arrangements'. *Urban Geography*, 1–4.

Roberts, S. and R. Schein. 1995. 'Earth Shattering: Global Imagery and GIS'. In *Ground Truth: The Social Implications of Geographic Information Systems*, ed. J. Pickles, 171–195. Guilford Press.

Sadowski, Jathan. 2020. 'Cyberspace and Cityscapes: On the Emergence of Platform Urbanism'. *Urban Geography*, 1–5.

Saïd, E. 1978. *Orientalism*. Vintage Books.

Samoilenko, Anna, Fariba Karimi, Daniel Edler, Jérôme Kunegis and Markus Strohmaier. 2016. 'Linguistic Neighbourhoods: Explaining Cultural Borders on Wikipedia through Multilingual Co-Editing Activity'. *EPJ Data Science* 5(1). https://doi.org/10.1140/epjds/s13688-016-0070-8.

Schech, Susanne. 2002. 'Wired for Change: The Links between ICTs and Development Discourses'. *Journal of International Development: The Journal of the Development Studies Association* 14(1): 13–23.

Schervish, Paul G. and John J. Havens. 1997. 'Social Participation and Charitable Giving: A Multivariate Analysis'. *Voluntas: International Journal of Voluntary and Nonprofit Organizations* 8(3): 235–260.

Schultz, Isaac. 2019. 'The Brief, Baffling Life of an Accidental New York Neighborhood'. *Atlas Obscura*, 2019. www.atlasobscura.com/articles/new-york-disappearing-neighborhood.

Sen, Shilad W., Heather Ford, David R. Musicant, Mark Graham, O.S. Keyes and Brent Hecht. 2015. 'Barriers to the Localness of Volunteered Geographic Information'. In *Proceedings of the 33rd Annual ACM Conference on Human Factors in Computing Systems*, 197–206.

Shahid, Abdul Rehman and Amany Elbanna. 2015. 'The Impact of Crowdsourcing on Organisational Practices: The Case of Crowdmapping'. ECIS 2015 Completed Research Papers. Paper 166.

Shapin, S. 1998. 'Placing the View from Nowhere: Historical and Sociological Problems in the Location of Science'. *Transactions of the Institute of British Geographers* 23(1):5–12.

Shaw, Joe and Mark Graham. 2017. 'An Informational Right to the City? Code, Content, Control, and the Urbanization of Information'. *Antipode* 49(4): 907–927.

Shelton, Taylor, Ate Poorthuis, Mark Graham and Matthew Zook. 2014. 'Mapping the Data Shadows of Hurricane Sandy: Uncovering the Sociospatial Dimensions of "Big Data"'. *Geoforum* 52: 167–179.

Shirky, Clay. 2011. 'The Political Power of Social Media: Technology, the Public Sphere, and Political Change'. *Foreign Affairs*, 28–41.

Shorrocks, Anthony, Jim Davies and Rodrigo Lluberas. 2015. 'Credit Suisse Global Wealth Report 2015'. Credit Suisse Research Institute.

Sinders, Caroline, Sydney Poore and Patrick Earley. 2018. 'Reporting Problems: A Survey Analysis of the Administrator's Noticeboard/Incidents on the English Wikipedia'. Wikimedia Foundation.

Smets, Annelien, Eladio Montero and Pieter Ballon. 2019. 'Does the Bubble Go Beyond?' ImpactRS '19, September 2019, Copenhagen, Denmark.

Soden, Robert and Leysia Palen. 2014. 'From Crowdsourced Mapping to Community Mapping: The Post-Earthquake Work of OpenStreetMap Haiti'. In *COOP 2014-Proceedings of the 11th International Conference on the Design of Cooperative Systems, 27-30 May 2014, Nice (France)*, 311–326. Springer.

Soeller, Gary, Karrie Karahalios, Christian Sandvig and Christo Wilson. 2016. 'Mapwatch: Detecting and Monitoring International Border Personalization on Online Maps'. In *Proceedings of the 25th International Conference on World Wide Web*, 867–878.

Spivak, Gayatri. 'The Rani of Sirmur'. *Barker* 1: 128–151.

Srnicek, Nick. 2017. 'The Challenges of Platform Capitalism: Understanding the Logic of a New Business Model'. *Juncture* 23(4): 254–257.

Stansfeld, Katherine. 2019. 'Mapping Multiplicity: Place, Difference and Conviviality in Finsbury Park, London'. PhD thesis, Royal Holloway University of London.

Stark, Hans-Jörg. 2011. 'Empirische Untersuchung Der Motivation von Teilnehmenden Bei Der Freiwilligen Erfassung von Geodaten'. *Fachhochschule Nordwestschweiz, Präsentation.*

Steinauer-Scudder, Chelsea. 2018. 'Counter Mapping'. *Emergence Magazine*, 2018. https://emergencemagazine.org/feature/counter-mapping/.

Stephens, Monica. 2013. 'Gender and the GeoWeb: Divisions in the Production of User-Generated Cartographic Information'. *GeoJournal* 78(6): 981–996.

Su, Hsi-Yao. 2003. 'The Multilingual and Multi-Orthographic Taiwan-Based Internet: Creative Uses of Writing Systems on College-Affiliated BBSs'. *Journal of Computer-Mediated Communication* 9(1): JCMC912.

Sui, Daniel and Michael Goodchild. 2011. 'The Convergence of GIS and Social Media: Challenges for GIScience'. *International Journal of Geographical Information Science* 25(11): 1737–1748.

Sumi, Róbert and Taha Yasseri. 2011. 'Edit Wars in Wikipedia'. In *2011 IEEE Third International Conference on Privacy, Security, Risk and Trust and 2011 IEEE Third International Conference on Social Computing*, 724–727. IEEE.

Sutton, Elizabeth. 2015. *Capitalism and Cartography in the Dutch Golden Age.* University of Chicago Press.

Takhteyev, Y. 2012. *Coding Places: Software Practice in a South American City.* MIT Press.

Tapscott, Don and Anthony D. Williams. 2006. *Wikinomics: How Mass Collaboration Changes Everything.* Print on demand.

Thebault-Spieker, Jacob, Loren G. Terveen and Brent Hecht. 2015. 'Avoiding the South Side and the Suburbs: The Geography of Mobile Crowdsourcing Markets'. In *Proceedings of the 18th ACM Conference on Computer Supported Cooperative Work & Social Computing*, 265–275.

Thompson, Peter and Melanie Fox-Kean. 2005. 'Patent Citations and the Geography of Knowledge Spillovers: A Reassessment'. *American Economic Review* 95(1): 450–460.

Touré, Hamadoun. 2012. 'U.N.: We Seek to Bring Internet to All'. *Wired*, 2012. www.wired.com/2012/11/head-of-itu-un-should-internet-regulation-effort/.

Unicode. 2018. 'Unicode Common Locale Data Repository'. 34b. http://cldr.unicode.org/.

Van der Velden, Maja. 2013. 'Decentering Design: Wikipedia and Indigenous Knowledge'. *International Journal of Human-Computer Interaction* 29(4): 308–316.

Vicario, Arnalie, David Garcia, Eugene Alvin Villar, Feye Andal, Maning Sambale, Mikko Tamura and Reynier Tasico. 2020. 'A Call to Correct Narratives about Geospatial Work in the Philippines'. A Statement by Members of the OpenStreetMap Philippines Community in Response to the "Philippines" Episode of Amazon Web Services' Documentary Series Now Go Build Which Highlights the Work of the Humanitarian OpenStreetMap Team in the Philippines. (blog). 2020. https://wiki.openstreetmap.org/w/images/a/aa/A_Call_to_Correct_Narratives_about_Geospatial_Work.pdf.

Vincent, Nicholas, Isaac Johnson, Patrick Sheehan and Brent Hecht. 2019. 'Measuring the Importance of User-Generated Content to Search Engines'. In *Proceedings of the International AAAI Conference on Web and Social Media* 13: 505–516.

Wade, Jess and Maryam Zainghalam. 2018. 'Why We're Editing Women Scientists onto Wikipedia'. *Nature*. 2018. www.nature.com/articles/d41586-018-05947-8.

Wadhwa, Kul and Howie Fung. 2014. 'Converting Western Internet to Indigenous Internet: Lessons from Wikipedia'. *Innovations: Technology, Governance, Globalization* 9(3–4): 127–135.

Wainwright, Joel. 2013. *Geopiracy: Oaxaca, Militant Empiricism, and Geographical Thought*. Palgrave Macmillan.

Warschauer, Mark, Ghada R. El Said and Ayman G. Zohry. 2002. 'Language Choice Online: Globalization and Identity in Egypt'. *Journal of Computer-Mediated Communication* 7(4): JCMC744.

Wiggins, Andrea and Kevin Crowston. 2010. 'Developing a Conceptual Model of Virtual Organizations for Citizen Science'. *International Journal of Organisational Design and Engineering* 1(1/2): 148.

——. 2011. 'From Conservation to Crowdsourcing: A Typology of Citizen Science'. In *2011 44th Hawaii International Conference on System Sciences*, 1–10. IEEE.

Wikimedia. 2017. '2017 Movement Strategy'. https://meta.wikimedia.org/wiki/Strategy/Wikimedia_movement/2017/Direction.

——. 2018. 'December 2018 Wikipedia Research Showcase'. www.youtube.com/watch?v=RKMFvi_CCB0.

——. 2019. 'Characterizing Wikipedia Reader Behaviour – Demographics and Wikipedia Use Cases'. Wikimedia Research. https://meta.wikimedia.org/wiki/Research:Characterizing_Wikipedia_Reader_Behaviour/Demographics_and_Wikipedia_use_cases.

——. 2021. 'Whose Knowledge?' In *Wikimedia Meta-Wiki*. https://meta.wikimedia.org/wiki/Whose_Knowledge%3F.

Wikipedia. 2021a. 'Wikipedia Edit-a-Thons'. https://en.wikipedia.org/wiki/Category:Wikipedia_edit-a-thons.

——. 2021b. 'WikiProjects Relevant for Countering Systemic Bias'. https://en.wikipedia.org/wiki/Category:WikiProjects_relevant_for_countering_systemic_bias.

Wilson, Matthew W. 2017. *New Lines: Critical GIS and the Trouble of the Map*. University of Minnesota Press.

Winichakul, Thongchai. 1994. *Siam Mapped: A History of the Geo-Body of a Nation*. University of Hawaii Press.

Wood, Harry. 2015. 'Sky News Interview – HOT Nepal Earthquake Mapping'. www.youtube.com/watch?v=DTH31Qgtu7o.

Yang, Chunsheng. 2007. 'Chinese Internet Language: A Sociolinguistic Analysis of Adaptations of the Chinese Writing System'. *Language@ Internet* 4(2).

Yang, Stephanie and Max Sklar. 2018. 'Finding the Perfect 10: How We Developed the Foursquare Venue Rating System'. *Foursquare* (blog). 2018. https://medium.com/foursquare-direct/finding-the-perfect-10-how-we-developed-the-foursquare-venue-rating-system-c76b08f7b9b3.

Yasseri, Taha, Robert Sumi, András Rung, András Kornai and János Kertész. 2012. 'Dynamics of Conflicts in Wikipedia'. *PloS One* 7(6): e38869.

Yates, Deborah and Leigh Dodds. 2018. 'How Facebook, Apple and Microsoft Are Contributing to an Openly Licensed Map of the World'.

The Open Data Institute (ODI). https://theodi.org/article/how-are-face book-apple-and-microsoft-contributing-to-openstreetmap/.

Zook, Matthew A. 2001. 'Old Hierarchies or New Networks of Centrality? The Global Geography of the Internet Content Market'. *American Behavioral Scientist* 44(10): 1679–1696.

Zook, Matthew A. and Mark Graham. 2007. 'Mapping DigiPlace: Geocoded Internet Data and the Representation of Place'. *Environment and Planning B: Planning and Design* 34(3): 466–482.

Zuboff, Shoshana. 2015. 'Big Other: Surveillance Capitalism and the Prospects of an Information Civilization'. *Journal of Information Technology* 30(1): 75–89.

Zukin, Sharon, Scarlett Lindeman, and Laurie Hurson. 2017. 'The Omnivore's Neighborhood? Online Restaurant Reviews, Race, and Gentrification'. *Journal of Consumer Culture* 17(3): 459–479.

Index

Note: *ct* refers to a chart; *ill* to an illustration; *t* to a table; *n* to a note; GM to Google Maps; WP to Wikipedia